DISEASES OF GLOBALIZATION
Socioeconomic Transitions and Health

Christine McMurray
and
Roy Smith

D1471833

EARTHSCAN

Earth~~scan Publications, London and Ster~~ling, VA

First published in the UK in 2001 by
Earthscan Publications Ltd

A catalogue record for this book is available from the British Library

ISBN: 1 85383 711 3 paperback
         1 85383 710 5 hardback

Typesetting by PCS Mapping & DTP, Newcastle upon Tyne
Printed and bound by Creative Print and Design Wales
Cover design by Richard Reid

For a full list of publications please contact:
Earthscan Publications Ltd
120 Pentonville Road
London, N1 9JN, UK
Tel: +44 (0)20 7278 0433
Fax: +44 (0)20 7278 1142
Email: earthinfo@earthscan.co.uk
http://www.earthscan.co.uk

22883 Quicksilver Drive, Sterling, VA 20166–2012, USA

Earthscan is an editorially independent subsidiary of Kogan Page Ltd and
publishes in association with WWF-UK and the International Institute for
Environment and Development

This book is printed on elemental chlorine-free paper

Contents

Preface

Modernization and globalization are characterized by increased linkages between states and groups within states. The emergence of a global economy has led to an erosion of sovereignty and local autonomy. An important consequence of the emphasis on liberal free-market economics has been a growing divide between those benefiting from and those disadvantaged by this process. This is reflected in divergent patterns of health and well-being.

Phenomena such as the free flow of capital and the growing incidence of transboundary pollution are examples of how governments and individuals can be affected by issues that are beyond their control. There has been a simultaneous process of the 'retreat of the state' in terms of welfare provision. Increasingly, development aims, such as meeting basic needs, are subsumed by a reliance on market forces as the key determinant in policy formation. Even where welfare provision is a stated government objective, the prescription tends to be to emphasize economic growth in the belief that such growth will benefit the whole of the community. The United Nations' (UN) Human Development Reports and similar studies indicate that even though there has been some progress in absolute poverty reduction, there are growing disparities, with many people receiving little benefit from economic growth. In particular this relates to varied experiences of health and well-being.

Although technological progress has brought the means to control infectious disease, some aspects of globalization have contributed to an increased risk of unhealthy lifestyles. All people are at risk, but marginalized groups are more likely to experience inferior living conditions and limited purchasing power. In addition to these economic and environmental constraints there are aspects of modernization that encourage the adoption of unhealthy lifestyles. These include stress, alienation and the aggressive marketing of fast foods, cigarettes and alcohol.

This book investigates the complex interactions between the micro and macro levels of structures and processes relevant to current trends of modernization. Case studies are used to illustrate the manner in which political change and economic modernization of marginalized communities has impacted on health and well-being. Mongolia, Uzbekistan and the Marshall Islands provide good examples of the various ways in which this occurs. We argue that these examples are illustrative of broader trends of modernization reflected throughout the world.

The study also explores the reasons why marginalized groups may *choose* to pursue unhealthy lifestyles, even when alternatives are possible. In-depth interviews with Marshallese reveal perceptions and attitudes that are at variance with popular explanations that their behaviour arises from ignorance and cultural preference. There is widespread awareness of the negative aspects of certain lifestyle habits, but the main factors precluding change are those arising from marginalization. This points to the need for an holistic approach to health that also addresses political and economic processes.

Chapters 1 to 4 provide a background to the manner in which a global political economy has developed. Several other discussions within fields such as international political economy or development studies have tended to focus on either the role of major financial institutions and their policies or the impact these have had on developing countries. Here we make reference to both of these aspects but our focus is on the spread of a particular model of development and modernization and how this brings both benefits and disadvantages to the communities involved in this process. Division of wealth is an obvious result of this process and is the underlying commonality within all recent reports on global trends. With this division arise varying opportunities to maintain health and well-being. Interestingly, there appears to be only a partial correlation between wealth and health. Clearly, extreme poverty has a negative impact on one's ability to maximize one's health and well-being. However, it appears that wealth in itself is no guarantee of good health. Quite the contrary in some instances, where ill health can be attributed to over- as opposed to under-consumption.

The above point is central to our argument. As described in Chapter 3 looking at determinants of health, we draw attention to several relevant factors. The macro level is significant in relation to broader international power relationships and the evolution of the core–periphery model of international trading and wealth creation.

At the national level there can be significant factors relating to domestic power relationships and the norms and values dominant within a particular society. Finally, the role of the individual as an agent within a range of structures is also considered. None of these levels should be seen as wholly distinct as they continually overlap and interact. Assessing which factors are significant in determining individuals' health and well-being requires an appreciation of this interaction.

The case studies chosen illustrate the potential significance of each of the above levels. All play some part in determining patterns of health and well-being. While acknowledging that there will be geographic, cultural and individual biological factors at play, our argument is that a key determinant is the process of modernization itself. As such, we highlight the shift in patterns of health within modernizing communities towards non-communicable diseases (NCDs) and lifestyle-related illnesses. This is enlightening for health provision in both developing and developed states. The core–periphery model adopted throughout this book applies equally well both between states and within them. Although the emphasis tends to be on the more marginalized members of communities it is also recognized that ill health impacts on the core states and even the most affluent members can suffer. Demographic trends suggest that the burden of health care will increase as a proportion of budgets within all states.

The genesis of this book was the authors' combined interests in the communities in the case study regions. However, it quickly became apparent that to understand what was happening within these communities we needed to take into account much broader issues relating to modernization and so-called globalization. Beyond that it was clear that if these communities were suffering ill health, partially as a consequence of adopting 'modern' or 'Western' aspirations and lifestyles, this also raises questions about this particular model of development. In turn this relates to more widespread patterns of health. A characteristic of modernization and the health transition is that people are living longer but require increased medical attention. By highlighting this transition within communities marginalized within the global political economy it is also the aim of this study to highlight similar patterns of ill health found within the core states.

Roy Smith, Nottingham, UK
Chris McMurray, Noumea, New Caledonia
January 2001

Acronyms and Abbreviations

CMEA	Council for Mutual Economic Assistance
DHS	Demographic and Health Survey (Uzbekistan)
FSM	Federal States of Micronesia
GATT	General Agreement on Tariffs and Trade
GDP	gross domestic product
HDI	Human Development Index
IMF	International Monetary Fund
IMR	infant mortality rate
IUD	intrauterine device
MOHE	Ministry of Health and Environment (RMI)
NCD	non-communicable disease
RMI	Republic of the Marshall Islands
STD	sexually transmitted disease
TFR	total fertility rate
TTPI	Trust Territories of the Pacific Islands
UN	United Nations
UNDP	United Nations Development Programme
UNICEF	United Nations International Children's Emergency Fund
USAKA	United States Army at Kwajalein Atoll (RMI)
WHO	World Health Organization
WTO	World Trade Organization

Chapter 1

The Issues

---

*'Health is a state of complete physical, mental and
social well-being, not merely the absence of disease or
infirmity'* (WHO Charter, 1946).

It is becoming increasingly evident that modernization is leading
to changing patterns of health. While there have been many
improvements in general population health, new health problems
have developed. Some are related to the adverse consequences of
industrialization, such as environmental contamination, some are
related to inadequate health care, and some are related to social
change and the development of unhealthy lifestyles. Certain
patterns of health tend to be consistently associated with certain
patterns of political and economic development. In particular,
there is a tendency for health and living standards to be lower
among those groups that have been marginalized by the process of
'globalization'; that is, various processes that undermine local
autonomy, such as international flows of capital and investments,
and the promotion of Western values and lifestyles through global
media transmissions. States and individuals have become intercon-
nected under the general rubric of 'globalization'. Many
communities have adopted the capitalist model of development
and patterns of consumption, even though they have maintained
distinctive cultures and characteristics. Not all, however, have
benefited equally from this process. For many people advances in
areas such as medical science and telecommunications have
brought undoubted benefits, but many others have been denied
such benefits.

A characteristic of globalization is that it facilitates uneven
growth. While some regions have become cores of economic

progress, others have been relegated to the periphery. Less developed health services in peripheral countries have slowed their progress in controlling infectious diseases. At the same time many peripheral countries are experiencing a rising incidence of NCDs related to a shift away from subsistence agriculture to a growing cash economy, urbanization and more sedentary lifestyles. There is evidence that these diseases are occurring at increasingly younger ages. This book is concerned with the ways in which globalization has fostered deteriorating health among some groups.

Our approach is cross-disciplinary. We consider aspects of sociology, economics, political science and health care. Such an approach is needed to make sense of the increasingly complex patterns of human behaviour that affect health. A key concern is the extent to which people are passive 'victims' of the processes of modernization and globalization, or, alternatively, openly embrace the perceived benefits of social and economic change. We therefore examine the levels of empowerment and the capacity of various groups to adopt healthier lifestyles, and the factors that limit their options.

We use examples from various countries to illustrate the key mechanisms through which globalization impacts on population health: quality of health services, environmental contamination and the adoption of new lifestyles. We look in detail at three case studies: Mongolia, Uzbekistan and the Republic of the Marshall Islands. Mongolia and Uzbekistan, which were in the former Soviet sphere of influence, are examples of countries where the main impacts on health have been related to industrialization and economic transition. Mongolia's population health has deteriorated in recent years because the health system has been severely disrupted by the transition to a market economy. Uzbekistan has experienced severe environmental contamination which has impacted on population health. At the same time it has experienced a deterioration of health services as a consequence of loss of Soviet budgetary assistance.

In the Western sphere of influence the Republic of the Marshall Islands serves as an example of one of the world's most geographically remote communities which has been inextricably drawn into the global economy, even though it has no industrial base. Although it has felt the impact of environmental contamination from nuclear testing, Marshallese health has also been profoundly affected by new patterns of aspiration, consumption and lifestyle resulting from contact with the USA. The Marshall Islands thus serves as our main example of the increase in lifestyle-related diseases in modernizing countries.

EXPANSION AND MARGINALIZATION

From the early works of Marx and Engels to contemporary political scientists such as Beck, there is a common theme of assessing the social implications of the driving forces of politics and the striving for economic growth.[1] Many have used the core–periphery model developed by Wallerstein, Myrdal and Frank.[2] Chomsky, Buchanan and others consider geographical and spatial dimensions of this model.[3] These can be any form of unequal relationship, whether based on the traditional analytical triumvirate of race, class and gender or other evolving social, economic and political classifications and divisions. Local cultures are increasingly overlaid by the influence of global economic forces. Robertson makes reference to a 'single space', a concept evolved from McCluhan's metaphor of a 'global village' and similar imagery suggesting time and space compression.[4] Advances in transport and telecommunications undoubtedly facilitate the interconnection of individuals and communities. A discipline of globalization studies has emerged in recent years in which writers such as Tomlinson discuss 'cultural imperialism'.[5] He argues that imposed Western values are coming into conflict with indigenous cultures around the world. The replacement of traditional subsistence practices by Western lifestyles that are deleterious to health is an example of this process.

International political and economic forces determine the lives of the world's population. In core–periphery terms this can be seen in the ongoing flow of resources from the least to the most developed states. The UN *Human Development Report 1997* states that the per capita income of the richest 20 per cent in industrial countries is 11 times that of South Asia.[6] Even greater disparities of wealth can be identified within states. An extreme example is that the richest Mexican in 1995 owned assets worth US$6.6 billion, which was equal to the combined income of the 17 million poorest Mexicans.[7] Similarly, the dominance of the key international financial institutions, The World Bank, the International Monetary Fund (IMF) and the World Trade Organization (WTO), by the most developed states also enhances the comparative advantage they enjoy in relation to the developing world. This is central to the pattern of development currently emerging. 'Free' trade is biased in favour of the most developed states. By removing trade barriers, the most developed states can use their multinational corporations to exploit economies of scale, to diversify investment and take advantage of cheap labour markets. Writers in the field of international political economy, such as Cox and Strange, have highlighted the significance of these structural elements within international relations.[8]

Since the end of the Cold War the most important international relations involve trade patterns, foreign direct investment and the flow of capital. The WTO has issued directives discouraging subsidies and tariff barriers. These directives are designed to prevent governments giving their goods an advantage in the international market place. This strategy assumes a 'level playing field' for international trade. Such a framework for trade does not exist; states operate within a hierarchical system, with some having a competitive advantage over others. The peripheral states are the most disadvantaged by this so-called free market system.

Frank described a process of 'development of underdevelopment'.[9] His arguments were based primarily on Latin America, but still have validity for all peripheral states and individuals. The process Frank describes suggests that although there can be mutual benefits from international trade they are almost always unequal in nature. Keohane and Nye's work on interdependence between states also highlights the inequality in international transactions.[10] Frank goes further in drawing attention to the flow of resources from periphery to core. He argues that in addition to being an unequal exchange, trade can actively undermine the development of the peripheral states. Given the complex mix of benefits from contact with core states, such as the opportunity for technology transfer, infrastructure improvements and possible education and employment opportunities, it is difficult to weigh the costs and benefits. Losses might include lack of control over commodity prices, an over-reliance on the export of primary resources and a lack of growth in domestic capital surpluses which are needed for more rapid economic and social development.

Chomsky takes the extreme position that there is a capitalist conspiracy towards global domination.[11] It is evident that there has been a widespread adoption of market-led policies reinforcing the ideology of capital accumulation. A symptom of this is that the most marginalized groups are those most likely to suffer ill health and are also those least able to improve their health. The key point is that structures exist that foster inequitable economic development. This includes the state itself, international economic institutions or even the ideological mind-set that since 'growth is good' policies should be driven by market forces as opposed to addressing basic needs.

Fukuyama draws attention to the dominance of liberal economics, particularly after the collapse of the Soviet Union and the end of the Cold War.[12] He argues that the failure of the Communist system under Soviet direction is symptomatic of the triumph of capitalism. There is certainly a strong argument that the spread of the capitalist system is self-reinforcing and, as such, will become increasingly difficult to displace with an alternative system. The capitalist model of development is having a tremendous influence on a global scale. This can be related to the types of lifestyle being increasingly adopted, and to the impact of social change on health.

Hagen argues that the main instigators of social change are those with the ability to become entrepreneurs, while others who lack the capacity or opportunity to become entrepreneurs are forced into 'retreatist' behaviour.[13] Global economic growth in recent years has brought increasing disparities in wealth. Growing numbers of people are failing to reap the benefits of modernization. Moreover, modern lifestyles involving varying degrees of individual choice, are actively contributing to poorer standards of health at older ages. Merton described a syndrome of retreatist behaviour, including excessive smoking and drinking and high rates of suicide, which have been observed in various marginalized communities in virtually all parts of the world.[14] This is sometimes a result of prejudice against certain groups. Such prejudices are influential in determining social standing and equality of opportunity.

The globalization of capital brings increasing numbers of people into its sphere of influence. Regardless of choice, or even willingness to participate, the world's population is feeling an increased impact from these global trends. A dramatic example of this is the projected sea-level rise associated with global warming due to industrialization. This is a process over which atoll dwellers in the Pacific have virtually no control, and yet, in a worst-case scenario, it could make many low-lying atolls and islands uninhabitable. In this example the potential negative impact is clear. More opaque are the effects of other factors such as fluctuating world commodity prices and the influence of imported television programmes, which are positive for some and negative for others. The global spread of such consequences of modernization sharpens the divide between the core dwellers and the peripheral and marginalized dwellers.

SHIFTING BOUNDARIES AND CHANGING VALUES

Core–periphery relationships are often fluid. A range of race, class and gender studies can be viewed as having a core–periphery structure. Classifications, or boundaries, shift according to the political, social or economic context in which a given scenario is enacted. An advantageous position with respect to one relationship can simultaneously be disadvantageous in another. Mapping core–periphery boundaries can thus involve overlapping complexities that vary depending on the focus of the analysis. For example, states may be defined as peripheral in relation to their respective superpower's or former superpower's sphere of influence, but the perceptions of some groups within each of the states referred to may differ depending on their own sense of identity, history and culture. Most individuals emphasize their nationality or their small group affiliation at different times, depending on their circumstances.

Despite strong national identities, the ability of people to act, such as in response to illness, is affected by their position in relation to the relevant core. The accessibility and affordability of health services are influenced by this relationship. On the one hand economic growth supports advances in medical treatments and other relevant science and technologies. On the other hand, globalization actively disadvantages growing numbers of people in terms of health and other aspects of well-being.

A general trend in the processes of modernization and globalization is increased urbanization and a growing dependence on the cash economy at a time when governments have declining control over international economic developments. When economic growth takes place the benefits do not necessarily 'trickle down' to the lower income sector. Often it has led to growing social segregation and the environmental degradation of marginal land. One of the great ironies of modernization is that there now exists the knowledge and capability to effect widespread improvements in the provision of basic needs and yet disparities in well-being are increasing. As indicated by the quotation from the World Health Organization (WHO) Charter at the beginning of this chapter, health is inextricably linked to political, economic and social issues and to distance from the core.

Modernization also affects health by changing values; for example, by devaluing the 'accumulated wisdom' of older generations. Although emotional attachment and societal expectations demand that provision is made to care for and support older generations, there is minimal financial return available from such expenditure. Traditional knowledge and skills may become irrelevant when new technologies and new methods of production are introduced. This may erode the customary norms and values of respect and deferment to elders. At the same time, the dominance of market forces in relation to most elements of community health raises the issue of whether care of the aged is the responsibility of the state or the family. This is an instance of market-led policies having social and cultural impacts.

THE DEMOGRAPHIC AND HEALTH TRANSITION

The process of modernization has also affected patterns of population change, which are fundamental to human welfare. Most industrialized countries have experienced the process of demographic transition, which is a shift from an almost stationary population balance with high fertility and mortality to another with low fertility and mortality. There is usually a period of substantial population growth in the interval between the first and second balance because mortality rates tend to decline before fertility rates.

In the 1940s, when demographic transition was first described, it was generally assumed that it was an automatic process that naturally accompanied modernization. It is now evident that, for various reasons, this theory is not a good explanation of patterns of population in some contemporary developing countries. In most of Europe, mortality decline was a slower process and more directly related to economic development than it has been in the post-war years. In contrast, many contemporary developing countries have experienced rapid declines as a result of the importation of modern medical technology such as immunization. However, fertility has declined only slowly, and the period of population growth has been sustained for so long that it is contributing to widespread poverty and can be seen as a serious obstacle to economic progress. The rate of population growth has become one of the most important concerns in the contemporary world.

One part of the process of demographic transition is health transition.[15] This refers to the changes in disease patterns and health-related behaviour associated with mortality decline. The key process of health transition is a reduction in the prevalence of infectious disease. Improved sanitation and hygiene, immunization, antibiotics and surgical advances are the main mechanisms. Spectacular declines in infant mortality have accounted for a substantial proportion of the increase in life expectancy. In most developed countries the risk of dying from epidemics is now small, and at the same time workplace hazards have been reduced significantly. The process of mortality decline took a century or more in European countries, but has occurred with astonishing rapidity in some other places. For example, life expectancy at birth in China was 47 years in 1960 but had increased to 70 years by 1988.[16]

The reduction of mortality from infectious diseases has been paralleled by an increase in NCDs. That is, instead of succumbing to infectious diseases at younger ages, people tend to die at older ages from NCDs, such as coronary malfunctions and cancer. Most people who reach age 70 or more die from an NCD as a consequence of the seemingly inevitable 'wearing out' of their biological systems. Thus, the shift in the cause of mortality from mostly infectious diseases to mostly NCDs is associated with an increase in life expectancy as a result of a general improvement in health. The shift towards NCDs has also placed an increased burden on health care budgets and generated an increased need for care of the aged.

The health transition is a very positive process in that it has reduced early death from infectious diseases. However, these benefits are being eroded by forces that promote a high prevalence of early-onset NCDs. That is, just as many contemporary developing countries have not made the demographic transition in the same way as industrialized countries, their health transition has also been different. In particular, an increasingly common pattern, especially among groups marginalized by globalization, is one of a high prevalence of both infectious diseases and NCDs. One of the main causes of this uneven progress in health is the impact of global capitalism and the way it has shaped lifestyles.

INFECTIOUS VERSUS NCDs

The nature of the disease pattern in any society has important implications as regards the type of health strategy adopted. From the point of view of health planners, there is a crucial difference between infectious and NCDs. Infectious diseases are spread primarily by contact with an infected person. This contact may be direct, such as when an individual comes close to or touches an infected person, or indirect, such as when an insect vector or a water source carries infectious material between people. Infectious diseases often occur as epidemics, and although some are associated with a particular age group, most affect people of all ages. A healthy individual may have a better chance of recovery, but will not necessarily be able to avoid contracting an infection unless they have already developed a specific immunity to it. Strategies to control the spread of infectious diseases therefore focus on immunizing populations against specific viruses, isolating infected cases and preventing transmission via water and insect vectors.

In contrast, the risk of developing NCDs is strongly associated with individual physical condition. Factors that increase the propensity to develop NCDs are termed 'lifestyle risk factors', and include lack of exercise, excess body weight, smoking and high rates of alcohol consumption. Individuals of any age whose resistance is weakened by one or more of these risk factors are more likely to develop NCDs than those who are not. In some instances an infectious disease may increase the risk of developing a specific NCD; for example, hepatitis B increases the risk of liver cancer, but more often NCDs occur independently of infection.

In addition to the above factors, the broader aspects of wealth distribution, in both a domestic and an international context, are also significant determinants of risk. This study recognizes that a lifestyle choice may have been adopted because of limitations in available options. For example, poor diet may be due to the unavailability or high market prices of particular foodstuffs. Lack of education could also play a role, and this too could be seen in terms of wealth and availability of educational opportunities.

Whereas the prevention of infectious disease is a relatively centralized activity, which can be tackled with broad-brush public health measures, the reduction of NCDs is largely the responsibility of individual citizens. Health authorities can do little more than provide health education and promote healthy lifestyles. No matter how much effort is put into health education campaigns, their success depends on the extent to which people adopt the healthy practices they are taught. Unfortunately, many factors can intervene to prevent people adopting healthy lifestyles, even when they are told about the importance of doing so. As a consequence, unhealthy lifestyle habits, including poor diets, insufficient exercise, smoking and heavy drinking, have become major causes of illness and death in most developed countries.

The connections between lifestyle, social position and health have long been recognized. Durkheim described social conditioning and response to social change,[17] while, more recently, the role of the social environment has been recognized as a factor influencing health.[18] The interface between individual action based on personal predisposition and influence of friends, family and broader societal factors is difficult to quantify. Brown and Harris described closed orders of Benedictine and Trappist monks with markedly different levels of blood cholesterol as a consequence of their differing dietary habits, but both with a much lower incidence of cardiovascular disease than males of equal age not living in monasteries. He concludes that the higher incidence to be found in the wider community was due to societal stress.

Unhealthy lifestyles lead to various costs, including loss of wages and salaries and loss of years of life, and also account for a large proportion of public health expenditure. Detailed statistics on the exact costs of unhealthy lifestyles are seldom available because a myriad of itemized costs would need to be considered, but rough estimates can be made on the basis of prevalence and rates of hospitalization and treatment. For example, in Australia, diet-related conditions such as cardiovascular disease, diabetes, osteoporosis and various cancers may absorb up to 20 per cent of the health budget.[19]

Other than the high costs of treating lifestyle-related illness, which must be borne to some extent by the community, the main impact of unhealthy lifestyles on developed societies tends to be at the individual level. They are less likely to present a significant obstacle to economic and social progress in countries with an abundance of educated labour. They are more of a problem in small countries or those where few people have the background and skills to govern and administer. For example, it may not be possible to replace senior politicians who are unable to function because of excess alcohol consumption, and they may lose credibility in international forums. This may disadvantage their country as they may be less able to attract foreign aid and investment. Also, since there is likely to be a strong hereditary element in leadership, it may not be possible for such a leader to delegate his or her responsibilities. Although politicians facing similar stresses will respond differently to such pressures, developing states face particular problems because they have limited human resource development.

Similarly, developing countries tend to have small percentages of the population in the wage labour force with high proportions of them employed in the government bureaucracy. A high incidence of lifestyle-related absenteeism is thus likely to lead to inefficiency in government agencies. In the competitive job markets of developed countries, officials whose lifestyle consistently interferes with their work performance are likely to lose their jobs. In small government departments jobs are obviously less specialized, and a single individual may perform various functions. If an official becomes dysfunctional the effect may be far reaching. In this way a healthy lifestyle becomes a relatively more important factor in the efficiency of the government process in developing nations. This situation may be aggravated where a relatively small group of officials are charged with attracting foreign aid and investment. These problems of having a limited human resource pool to draw on can apply equally in small or in larger developing countries where the supply of qualified professional personnel is limited.

It is generally held that, within developed societies, economically and socially disadvantaged people are more likely to have unhealthy lifestyles, whereas educated people are more likely to be aware of health risks and live a healthier lifestyle.[20] However, the reverse may be true in societies where the bulk of the population is living a subsistence lifestyle. In such societies the leaders and senior officials have higher incomes and greater exposure to Western lifestyles than the majority of the population. Although some continue to live a modest and abstemious lifestyle and retain good health throughout their lives, many others acquire high-risk lifestyle behaviours. This may be, in part, a consequence of work-related stress.

During the initial phase of modernization it is probable that elite groups will adopt some of the high-risk behaviours of modern life, because of their new experiences and responsibilities which they are likely to find stressful. Again, this illustrates the point that boundaries may vary with different perspectives and experiences. A relatively high level of income does not necessarily signify a healthy lifestyle, but it does signify a wider range of options than a low income. Similarly, even those with a good level of education and good understanding of what constitutes a healthy lifestyle may adopt unhealthy habits. The USA is a world leader in terms of income and education, yet even here there are growing incidences of early-onset NCDs.

Unhealthy lifestyles are costly because they erode the human resource base and the illnesses they cause require expensive treatments. Most developing countries are less able to afford the high costs of managing NCDs. Where resources are limited, the opportunity cost of investing in health care is usually investment in economic and social development. Lifestyle may thus present a significant barrier to economic and social progress.

This book is concerned with the impact of modernization and globalization on health. Identifying the mechanisms that cause modernization to have negative impacts on health is an important step towards making effective policy to alleviate these problems. Our study differs from previous studies of health and lifestyles in that it considers individual and community level factors as well as global level factors. Individuals respond to the range of lifestyle options and choices available in any community, which, in turn, is determined by international relations and global influences. The following pages therefore look not only at the choices people make but also at the options available to them, which are determined by the broader political, economic and environmental context.

Chapter 2

Equity, Sustainability and Modernization

The processes of modernization and globalization have varying impacts on communities and individuals. This is particularly true in relation to living standards, patterns of health, the provision of health care services and attitudes towards health. This chapter focuses on the impact of global development on societal health and well-being. For some people the process of modernization leads to impoverishment while others prosper.

There are various perceptions of poverty. Impoverishment implies a reduction from one category to another, but the categories may overlap and an individual may be fulfilled in one category but poor in another.

'BOTTOM-UP' AND 'TOP-DOWN' APPROACHES TO DEVELOPMENT

There is a wealth of opinions on what constitutes development, what its aims should be and how they should be met. Few would argue against the objective of meeting the world population's basic needs and improving living standards. Some ecologists may raise doubts about the dominant position assigned to humans in relation to other species, but there is a general consensus that human well-being should be maximized. There are also different views about how development should be achieved, about the role of market forces and whether to approach development from the 'bottom-up' or 'top-down'. A fundamental aspect of this debate is the level of state intervention deemed appropriate.

There are three main approaches to development. Early capitalism was predominantly market-driven and relied primarily on economic growth to promote societal well-being. Generally, minimal investment was made in welfare provision although some industrialists in the UK, such as George Cadbury and Joseph Rowntree, improved their workers' living conditions. This can be viewed as a combination of altruistic philanthropy and sound business acumen in human resource investment. Subsequently a modified capitalist approach evolved in which the basic capitalist system was tempered with some welfare measures. In the early 1900s New Zealand was at the forefront of welfare legislation with the introduction of pensions, universal free education and universal suffrage. A third approach to development is pure socialism in which the central objective is to provide all citizens with basic needs, with all surpluses taken by the state. Various communist regimes have taken this approach. Although it is fundamentally different from the capitalist approach some define it as state capitalism.

The key difference between these three approaches to development is the mechanisms they use to achieve their objective. The socialist countries promote a 'bottom-up' approach in which the focus of development is the community. Everyone is involved in some way, either directly as production workers or by providing services to the community. In return they receive all the basic necessities for life from the state. This may or may not involve cash transfers. In contrast, capitalist systems adopt a 'top-down' approach in which the provision of basic needs occurs indirectly as a spin-off of development. Employment is not automatic but investment and development create job opportunities. By obtaining employment, individuals can earn the means to purchase the basic needs for themselves and their dependants.

However, a 'top-down' approach does not necessarily bring employment to those most in need. For example, the construction of gigantic dams in Africa during the 1960s and 1970s, which were symbols of national pride, had negative rather than positive impacts on substantial numbers of people. Ghana's Volta, Egypt's Aswan and Zimbabwe's Kariba, among others, were all massive, capital intensive projects. Although they improved the electricity supply and irrigation capacity of the surrounding regions, the flooding of valleys displaced thousands, most of whom received no direct benefit, but rather were economically marginalized by the dam construction. In addition, some dams spread diseases such as bilharzia and malaria, and others brought food shortages and social disruption with its associated problems of stress-related illness and self-destructive behaviour. Timberlake points out that the real need was not for large dams but for small irrigation dams to benefit local communities rather than consumers of electricity who were mostly urban based; that is, a 'bottom-up' rather than a 'top-down' approach. Although agencies such as the World Bank no longer tend to promote dam building projects on this scale, there are still repercussions from the construction of these dams.[1]

Capitalist, welfare capitalist and socialist approaches to development all have elements of inequality. The capitalist system inevitably produces inequality because different types of economic activity yield different returns and some individuals and groups have more opportunities to accumulate wealth. Even in socialist systems some people receive superior services and other benefits. The quality of, and access to, services varies between urban and rural areas and between core and peripheral states. Moreover, the overall standard of services is often below that of wealthier free market economies. Similarly, in the welfare state those who depend on welfare may be disadvantaged in terms of the quality and quantity of services they receive. Within all three systems those who are in positions of power and influence are better off.

Although cheap labour assists economic growth, the presence of large numbers of people who are unable to meet their own needs is counter productive in any economic system. Poverty is expensive. It increases the demand for whatever health and welfare services are available and diverts revenue away from the improvement of infrastructure and investment in further production. The UN *Human Development Report 1997* highlights remarkable achievements in global economic growth, yet points out that poverty remains pervasive. Roughly one-third of the world's population live on incomes of less than US$1 a day.[2] Although such figures are open to many interpretations they indicate that the assumption that growth will eventually 'trickle down' to all levels of society, is unrealistic.

Marginalization of states or groups within states can be linked to patterns of uneven development. The impacts of free-market driven development are tremendously diverse. As more activities become monetarized the need for a reliable cash income becomes increasingly important. Those in the higher income brackets have little trouble affording their basic needs. Their concerns are how to maintain their income, assuming goods are available. Those who do not have a reliable income are at risk of deteriorating living standards. Most of the developed states are experiencing a 'retreat of the state', as increasing demands for high-standard welfare services are becoming unaffordable for governments. Accordingly they are reducing expenditure in this sector and promoting privatization of areas such as health care and pension schemes. For those unable to reap financial benefits from modernization the trend towards the privatization of services leads to progressive marginalization and relative disadvantage.

It is important to recognize that, although there is growing homogenization of experience around the world with respect to the type of developments occurring, there is a simultaneous divergence of experience between those who benefit from modernization and those who do not. Within states there is often a spatial dimension to inequality; urban ghettos and shanty towns have lower living standards and inadequate welfare systems, particularly where neo-colonial economies are operating.

With respect to lifestyle, health and health care, this divergence is most accurately depicted in terms of the options available. This applies at the level of both the individual and the governments operating within an increasingly liberal and competitive global economy.

There are undoubted benefits of modernization. Break-throughs in medical science, telecommunications, manufacturing processes, computing and many other fields of endeavour have vastly increased human capacity to understand and manage a wide range of issues. Research into genetic engineering has the potential to alter the way we look at life itself. Yet for all of these developments it remains the case that basic needs are not being met in many parts of the world. Even in the most developed states instances of extreme poverty can be identified. Current patterns of development suggest that optimal health is not being achieved among many marginalized groups and individuals. The reasons can be found in the current patterns of exploitation and disadvantage faced by those marginalized from the potential benefits of modernization.

The following section looks at the extent to which individuals and governments have the capacity to influence current trends in modernization. This is important to establish the determinants of modernization and the way in which they may be influenced or controlled.

MONO-DEVELOPMENT AND CHOICE

With the collapse of the Soviet Empire, the ideological counter to Western capitalism, there is a popular view that 'the West has won' and a particular model for development has proved supreme. For those who have benefited from this system there is ample evidence to suggest that things are going well, with increased standards of living and a growing selection of consumer goods available for purchase. Those who have been marginalized are clearly in a different category.

The Brandt Report argued that in the longer term there is an interdependent relationship operating within the global political economy, whereby the developed states need the underdeveloped for primary resources and as markets for manufactured goods.[3] This implies that there can be some 'wastage' of people on the periphery without harming the interests at the core. The emphasis is on maintaining control of key structures and processes. The spread of a single model for development reinforces this control.

The equity and sustainablity of a global model of development raises two issues in relation to the provision of health care and the growing incidence of lifestyle-related illness. First, to what extent is inequity inherent within this system? Given that the whole basis of liberal capitalism is the accumulation of wealth, it inevitably leads to inequalities which tend to increase in scale, both within and between societies. One way in which these inequalities can be measured relates to patterns of health and access to health care services.

Second, can such a system be sustained over a long period of time? Projected outcomes vary depending on the timeframe adopted, the definition of sustainability, and beliefs, such as that economic growth increases equity. Differing forecasts depend on the forecaster's perspective and position within the economic system.

In recent decades it has been demonstrated that the capitalist system can perpetuate itself at the expense of marginalized groups and individuals. This has been accompanied by growing concerns that the ecosystem is under increasing pressure from industrialization and non-sustainable development practices. In the early 1970s there were numerous predictions regarding the availability of fossil fuels.[4] Due to alterations in pricing and the discovery of additional resources these predictions are generally now considered to be underestimates. Yet the basic argument concerning the non-sustainability of this type of energy production and its associated pollution still holds true. Timeframes for global degradation are now usually presented not in terms of when resources will be depleted, but in terms of how long the ecosystem can absorb the levels of pollution caused by fossil fuels. Views are variously optimistic or pessimistic. Those who believe in a 'technical fix' to pollution problems speak of ongoing growth and advancement. More pessimistic observers predict a dramatic collapse, or a series of evolving crises such as famine, climate change or armed conflict over shrinking resources.

For those who are marginalized within the global economy, crisis has already arrived. Already there are areas of the world that are so degraded that they are unlikely to fully recover. An example is the Aral Sea region, discussed later in this book. These marginalized environments and the communities living in them are currently experiencing the 'crisis of capitalism'. In some instances the term crisis might not seem appropriate; for example, in the difference between a famine situation and one where there is endemic malnutrition. Similarly, the high prevalence of lifestyle-related disease may not have as high a profile as death caused by natural disaster or cataclysmic event. Yet it remains the case that many such diseases are life-threatening. They can also reduce both length and quality of life. Diabetes, for example, may not lead to immediate death, but there can be symptoms which result in disabilities such as loss of sight or amputation. In addition to the suffering caused to individuals this also burdens health care services.

EXPLOITATION BY TRADE

The creation of the WTO is the clearest indication to date of an institutionalized global economy. It symbolizes economic patterns of exchange that have inexorably developed to the point whereby any economic analysis can only be fully understood if it is set within the context of broad global forces. To some extent the WTO can be seen as a natural progression from the World Bank, the IMF and the General Agreement on Tariffs and Trade (GATT). Moreover, it has reinforced previous flows of wealth and drawn greater numbers of the world's population into the cash economy.

The spread of consumerism and the promotion of Western goods in developing countries has assisted the global economy by ensuring a supply of primary produce. The desire for cash with which to purchase consumer goods encourages rural producers in developing countries to divert some of their effort into the production of cash crops. For example, in western Kenya many smallholders grow sugar on a contract basis and reserve little of their land for food cultivation. Although in a good year this enables them to benefit from increased purchasing power, they are vulnerable to crop failures and price fluctuations. When conditions are bad they may not only lose their cash incomes but may also find themselves with an inadequate supply of food.[5] There are many other examples of communities endangering their food security by adopting cash cropping, such as coffee growers in Papua New Guinea and tobacco smallholders in Zimbabwe. In the Solomon Islands the sale of logging rights has led to environmental degradation and loss of the environment which previously supported a subsistence lifestyle.

ENVIRONMENTAL CONTAMINATION

Core–periphery patterns of trade have also led to exploitation in terms of degradation of land and other environmental pollution. Many parts of the world have suffered environmental pollution due to the negative consequences of colonial relationships or the transfer of toxic wastes and 'dirty' industries to developing countries. One of the reasons for improved living standards in the developed states is that there has been legislation introduced to reduce environmental pollution. As a result, several of the pollution-creating processes in manufacturing and the disposal of waste products have been exported to developing states. The manner in which this is done varies and can be with the approval of the states receiving such waste. However, they may be forced to accept such industries and wastes because they desperately need external revenue and have limited opportunities to acquire it. It is quite likely that as a result of domestic core–periphery relations, those who agreed to such arrangements would not be the people who suffered the more negative consequences. For example, the government officials responsible for accepting toxic wastes would be unlikely to reside near the allocated dump site.

Contamination of land is a basic disadvantage for marginalized people. It not only devalues property but also sets a standard of value for inhabitants. This might not be a self-assessment but rather how they are regarded by other members of their society. Perceptions of a person's value or social standing tend to be linked to the area in which they reside. This can have implications for personal relationships, job opportunities and resulting income potential. It can also lead to a spiral of decline in which there is little or no motivation to restore the environment once it has become littered or polluted. This, in turn, may lead to low self-esteem and self-destructive lifestyle habits. Although lifestyle-related illness can be found across social class divisions there is a preponderance among lower income groups.

Illness and disease can arise in relation to both lifestyle habits and physical environment. If one resides on contaminated land it may cause ill health, regardless of other aspects of lifestyle. Taking adequate exercise or eating a healthy diet are no protection against incidents such as the Chernobyl nuclear accident, or the poisonous gas clouds released from the Union Carbide plant in Bhopal. These two examples illustrate the potential for pollution associated with industrialization. In both instances the spread of pollution was relatively indiscriminate, although in the case of Bhopal the incidence of ill health was intensified as the gas cloud passed over an area of inadequate housing where it was difficult to seek shelter. In this example low income added to the negative impact of this particular pollutant. Generally, lower income housing is more likely to be situated close to factories or dump sites which represent greater health risks. Similarly there is likely to be poor sanitation and an increased risk of contracting infectious diseases in such locations.

UNEVEN SOCIAL DEVELOPMENT

The societal divisions that arise from uneven development are mutually reinforcing. Once marginalized to poor land, limited opportunities and an increased risk of ill health it is increasingly difficult to gain a foothold in the economy of success. In a model of development that focuses on economic growth, investment is likely to coalesce at the higher end of the economic spectrum. There tends to be a far greater return from income-generating business investment as opposed to, for example, a health care centre. Again this reflects a particular approach to development with the emphasis firmly on economic growth, which may or may not feed through to the lower income strata of society.

Societies retain norms and values that have points of reference beyond material wealth. Status associated with blood line or other forms of celebrity can survive the shift to a cash economy. However, as cash economies develop, disposable income becomes a more important determinant of access to an increasing number of services. In relation to health, income also affects the probability of becoming ill and the means by which good health can be restored.

In addition to marginalizing poorer sectors of society, uneven development has a significant impact on the higher income groups. It entrenches their position, as capital accumulation enables them to enjoy comparative advantages in virtually all aspects of socio-economic interaction. Wealth can determine major differences between individuals. Within urban areas rich and poor can live in close proximity, yet clear divides remain. In London or New York rich and poor can live on the same street, but one may not be housed. Outside of sharing some space, their lives can be quite separate with different access to a whole range of services, including health care. As one moves to areas less integrated into modernization there can still be disparities of wealth and opportunity but they tend to be less stark. All societies are hierarchical to some degree. However, with modernization and the increased consumption of goods, it is becoming more readily apparent where one stands in society, at least in terms of material wealth.

Technological innovation has a disproportionate effect on the potential divisions between rich and poor. Access to computer facilities, advanced telecommunications systems and all manner of labour-saving devices provides not only a more secure lifestyle for the wealthy but also reinforces their position in relation to the broader society. Technological progress also means that higher levels of education and skills are required in order to obtain employment in the modern sector. At the same time, much new technology can be used only in states and regions where there has been investment in the necessary infrastructure such as reliable electricity systems and transport links.

Modernization is dynamic and constantly evolving as new discoveries are made and new products enter the market place. Usually the innovations are, at least initially, beyond the reach of the lower income groups. These groups, thus, continually fall behind the wealthy, who continue to reap the benefits of modernization. The dynamic process of modernization, however, refers back to questions raised earlier regarding sustainability. How likely is it that the lifestyles enjoyed by the wealthy can be either maintained or expanded to encompass greater numbers? This question is especially relevant in relation to global patterns of consumption and the logical inconsistencies of global capitalism.

PATTERNS OF CONSUMPTION

Questions about sustainability relate to population growth and patterns of consumption. Broadly speaking, there are two schools of thought. First, there are those that fear an impending crisis due to population growth and a resulting depletion of resources. The counter view is that the world could support considerably more people if resources were utilized more equitably.

Both of these views are partially correct. The alarmists are right to draw attention to the dramatic increase in the world's population. Although it took until AD 1800 to reach the first billion, the second billion was reached in the 1920s. Since then the world's population has trebled. A recent slowing of growth rates has caused the UN to revise projections downward, but it is still almost inevitable that the world's population will reach 8 billion and likely that it will exceed 10 billion before stabilizing.[6] Such a massive increase in numbers must severely deplete resources even if developing countries do not increase their per capita levels of consumption. Since resources of raw materials and productive land are finite, the capacity to increase consumption is limited, even allowing for more equitable patterns of consumption. This assumes a radical alteration in both existing patterns of wealth and future economic policies, and also a limit to population growth.

Existing patterns of consumption have a clear geographical dimension, with by far the greatest consumption taking place in the industrialized nations. For example, there is a vast disparity in the amount of waste produced by individuals in different parts of the world. It has been estimated that in developing states the average amount of waste produced in a year per person equals 150 times their body weight. This compares with 1000 times for the average European and 3900 times for a citizen of the USA. Similar ratios have been cited for the consumption patterns of various mineral resources.[7] Clearly if all those in the developing world matched the consumption and wastage levels averaged in the USA there would be a rapid depletion of the world's resources.

There are two distinct reactions to such observations, related to country of origin. Those from the industrialized countries are likely to argue that it would be impossible for the rest of the world to emulate their lifestyle and therefore restrictions should be placed on their rate of modernization, industrialization, economic growth and consumerism. In contrast, those from developing states argue that the industrialized world should reduce its consumption pattern to more manageable proportions. From the developing states' perspective there is a degree of hypocrisy in the developed world's position of modernizing, often at the expense of their colonial territories, and subsequently denying similar advances to other states. For example, Malaysia's President Mahatia has firmly stated this view.

Although some would go as far as to say that the developed states are actively surpressing development in the newly industrializing states, it is difficult to prove a grand conspiracy. None the less, there is a vocal and often acrimonious debate regarding the level of development considered appropriate in various parts of the world. This debate is played out in a range of international forums. A significant forum for discussing development policies is provided by the Earth Summit initiative. Following the 1992 UN Conference on Environment and Development in Rio there have been ongoing negotiations regarding the emission of greenhouse gases, loss of biodiversity, management of forests and a range of issues related to conservation and development. One of the noticeable characteristics of these negotiations is the tension that exists between developed and developing states. Again this relates to patterns of consumption and the perceived inequity of what appears to be a double standard with regard to acceptable levels of consumption and pollution. By focusing on economic growth the developing states often sacrifice environmental protection and other aspects of welfare.

The WTO's proposals for an increasingly liberal global economic regime and the removal of tariffs and trade barriers were claimed to create a level playing field in terms of competition. However, the developed states have an advantage in terms of scientific advancement and multinational corporations that can shift investment around the world virtually at will. Developing states may have cheaper labour costs, but overall they operate from a disadvantaged position, and usually lag behind the more developed states in terms of wealth generation. This applies beyond the level of government.

Consumerism has spread into many developing states and Western consumer goods have become widely accepted and sought after. In some developing states businesses have arisen producing counterfeit goods to meet this demand. Despite an obvious dilemma in matching disposable income to the availability of goods, when they have the means many people in the developing world appear enthusiastic to 'buy into' such consumption patterns. For example, Western designed household appliances can be found all over the world and Western food retailers such as McDonald's have become popular even in some socialist countries such as China. An indication of the popularity of Western fast foods is that although their relative cost is often much higher than in the core Western countries there is a very strong demand for them and they have even become a status symbol.

Assuming that the dominant, curative model of development remains that adopted around the world, the prospects for an equitable division of the benefits of sustainable modernization seems poor. As resources become further depleted it seems logical to assume that there will be increased competitiveness in markets with increased prices and more noticeable divisions between the haves and have nots. The process of marginalization is likely to become more extreme. The following chapter examines the mechanisms through which marginalization increases the risk of poor health and lifestyle-related illness.

Chapter 3

The Determinants of Health

Differences in health and longevity are important manifestations of socioeconomic differences between and within core and peripheral countries. There have been dramatic changes in the patterns of health and illness in the more developed countries. As described in Chapter 1, the original European health transition was triggered by improvements in sanitation and hygiene. The subsequent development of safe surgical procedures, immunization and modern drug therapies, especially antibiotics, sustained a gradual transition to a low incidence of infectious diseases. As increasing numbers survived until old age there was a relative increase in NCDs as a cause of death. Transitions such as those of East Asia occurred much more rapidly when a range of health measures, which had taken a century or more to be developed in Europe, were introduced almost simultaneously.[1]

In recent years it has become increasingly common for contemporary developing countries and countries in economic transition to experience a piecemeal health transition rather than to replicate the experiences of the industrialized countries. This is often related to a demographic transition that is also different from the European model, in that fertility is much slower to decline than mortality, so there is a longer period of population growth. Many contemporary countries are finding their sustained population growths are hindering economic development and limiting the availability of capital for investing in the improvement of living conditions and health services. This leads to uneven progress in health, with a mixed pattern of both infectious and NCDs as the major causes of death, and differing access to health facilities within countries.

Uneven progress in health can be found in many contemporary developing countries. Even though most have experienced a marked reduction in mortality from infectious diseases, a substantial proportion of deaths are still caused by illnesses that could be prevented or cured by existing medical technology. For example, in many developing countries high percentages of young children are immunized against six or seven major diseases, but others die from infectious conditions such as diarrhoea and respiratory diseases. Although there may be no readily available vaccines for these conditions, they could be prevented, or their incidence could be greatly reduced, by investment in improved living standards. There is also an increasing tendency for NCDs to occur among those who are only in their 40s and 50s or even younger. Even if these early-onset NCDs are not an immediate cause of death, they often contribute to a premature death and reduce aspects of well-being.

Uneven progress in health within countries also manifests as substantial differences between rich and poor, and between residents of different regions, in their living standards and their access to health care. Although most countries subscribe to the 1978 Alma Ata conference objective of 'Health for All by the Year 2000',[2] when health resources are scarce, rich countries can provide better access to health care for more of their populations.

Progress in health is determined by many factors, which interact to determine the risk of contracting a given illness at any point in time, and the chances of being cured. So many things impact on health that some grouping is necessary to facilitate discussion and analysis, although there are countless linkages both within and between groups of factors. The main determinants of health can be grouped in various ways. The needs of our study are best served by a simple classification into three groups, which we will call genetic, external and sociological.

Genetic factors determine the physical endowment of individuals. They comprise a set of inherited physical characteristics, including ethnic and family characteristics, inherited risk factors and sometimes congenital defects or illnesses. Aside from a discussion of a possible genetic propensity for obesity among some populations, genetic factors are not a central concern of this book. It is assumed here that all populations have roughly the same potential for health and longevity, and differences at the population level are, for the most part, due to variations in external and sociological factors.

External factors are the characteristics of the surroundings in which individuals and communities exist. They include the physical environment, climate, water quality and agricultural productivity, the political context, economic conditions, rural or urban residence and the availability and quality of health care. External factors affect health directly by determining exposure to disease and the chances of being cured, and indirectly by determining the range of lifestyle options available to individuals and communities.

The third group, sociological factors, shape the lifestyle choices made by individuals and communities. They include cultural and social norms, and behaviours which shape responses to a given set of external factors. The range of options available to individuals and groups is determined by the external factors, while the choices they make from these options are determined by sociological factors. Obviously there are no sharp divides between these groups, as sociological factors clearly play a role in shaping external factors, and vice versa. This grouping is therefore used only to facilitate analysis of the relative importance of the factors shaping options and the factors shaping choices at any given point in time or in any given situation.

Population size and structure are also related to health patterns. Population is a fundamental determinant of economic conditions, while at the same time it is shaped by economic and sociological factors. As an underlying factor it does not fit readily into either group and must be considered separately.

POPULATION CHARACTERISTICS AND PATTERNS OF HEALTH

The main population characteristics that affect health are absolute population size, growth rates, age structure and the ratio of workers to dependants. Population size must be evaluated in relation to the wealth generated from the exploitation of resources or from activities such as commerce. Wealthy countries can provide high living standards for relatively large populations, whereas even a relatively small population may lead to a state of 'over population' if few resources are available. For example, the state of Singapore's strong economy, which is built on manufacturing and trade, supports a population of 3 million on a very small land area with negligible natural resources. In contrast, 10 million people living on the vast but resource poor territory of Niger are relatively impoverished.

Population growth rates affect the rate of increase in demand for services. Although moderate population growth rates can stimulate economic growth by providing an expanding market, rapid growth rates quickly erode economic gains. Following its separation from Pakistan, Bangladesh experienced rapid population growth which soon transformed the wealthy state of Bengal into one of the poorest nations in the world. Even after a substantial decline in fecundity Bangladesh is still experiencing difficulty in raising per capita incomes and living standards.

As well as absolute numbers, the age structure of a population has important implications for economic progress. Age structure determines the ratio of working age to non-working age population, known as the age dependency ratio, and the type of services required. Populations with high fertility and large percentages of children below working age have relatively few workers compared with non-workers, but generate a strong demand for maternal and child health services and education. Although the burden of large numbers of dependants may slow the rate of economic growth, in the long run young populations provide an expanding labour force and generate a strong demand for employment as young people reach working age. This may be an advantage where there is high potential for economic growth, but failure to expand employment fast enough to absorb school leavers produces unemployment in the working age groups. In such instances the ratio of non-income earners to income earners increases and opportunities for capital accumulation decline. Where state-funded welfare systems are limited or non-existent, families must take on the burden of caring for dependants of working age. Although this may not be a great hardship where families can produce their own food, it can be very burdensome for those living in urban areas, or for the landless rural populations.

Populations with a more balanced age structure have relatively less demand for maternal and child health services and are capable of higher rates of capital accumulation, because of lower dependency ratios. This generates favourable conditions for rapid economic growth, improved living standards and longer life expectancies. However, in the long term the dependency ratio may increase as more people survive beyond working age. This, in turn, increases the demand for services for the non-working population, but in this instance the main need is for aged care rather than maternal and child health services. Since populations with long life expectancies tend to die of degenerative conditions such as cancer and coronary disease, aged care may involve long periods of hospitalization and costly medical services. This, too, can be a substantial drain on an economy, and many contemporary developed countries are taking steps to spread the burden of aged care by promoting privatization of health care and medical insurance schemes.

Different population patterns are associated with particular health patterns and health service requirements. High population growth rates and large percentages below working age tend to be associated with low per capita incomes and high prevalence of infectious diseases. States with high age dependency ratios often find it difficult to expand essential services sufficiently to keep pace with population growth and to ensure safe living environments, so they are slow to make the health transition. Many African states fall into this category, with high prevalence of infectious diseases, which could be controlled with existing medical technology if the government could afford appropriate levels of health care.

Ageing populations are associated with higher living standards, lower prevalence of infectious disease and increasing prevalence of NCDs at advanced ages. As the age structure shifts from predominantly young to increasingly old, infectious diseases are likely to be controlled, there is a reduction in demand for maternal and child health services and an increasing demand for aged care. In most developed countries the shift has been so gradual and there has been sufficient economic growth that they have adjusted to and coped with the requirements of the changing age balance. In extreme cases, however, such as China, a rapidly changing age structure has presented problems. After rapidly and dramatically reducing its fertility rate, China is now facing the problem of caring for a projected 300 million people over the age of 65. Even though the lower fertility rate has helped China to achieve rapid economic progress in recent years, this new age dependency ratio poses a formidable problem.

Population size and composition, thus, have several indirect impacts on health. At the national level the overall size and structure of a population affects health by affecting the rate of economic progress and the capacity of the country to provide health services.

Age structure also determines the mix of health services required. Similarly, at the household level family size, structure and the dependency ratio affect income, well-being and the demand for services.

EXTERNAL FACTORS AS DETERMINANTS OF HEALTH

Economic conditions are perhaps the most fundamental underlying determinants of health. It is a truism to say that top people live longer. Countless studies have shown an association between life expectancy, wealth and social status, both at the national and at the individual level. Compendia of national statistics, such as those produced by the World Bank, United Nations International Children's Emergency Fund (UNICEF) and United Nations Development Programme (UNDP), clearly show that countries with low per capita incomes have high levels of under-five mortality and short life expectancies. For example, UNICEF data for 1994 show that average life expectancy at birth for the ten countries with the lowest average per capita incomes was 48 years. For the ten with the highest per capita incomes it was 77 years.[3]

Real gross domestic product (GDP) per capita, life expectancy and educational attainment are indicators used by UNDP to calculate its Human Development Index (HDI).[4] In the country with the lowest HDI value in 1997, Sierra Leone, 52 per cent of the population as at 1990 were not expected to survive to age 40. The figure exceeded 30 per cent for all but three of the 20 countries with the lowest index values. In contrast, the average for the top 20 countries was 3.2 per cent.[5] Similarly, numerous studies have shown large and persistent differences in mortality between socio-economic groups, within both developed countries[6] and developing countries.[7]

There are several mechanisms through which economic conditions affect health and survival. At the individual and community level they determine the basic essentials of life: nutrition, housing and quality of the environment. Within countries, individual economic circumstances determine control over resources and ability to access health facilities. Even in the poorest countries the wealthiest groups can enjoy a healthy lifestyle. The poorest of cities, such as Maputo in Mozambique and Dar es Salaam in Tanzania, can provide potable tap water in their five star hotels for those who are able to pay for it. Higher income groups are more able to afford spacious houses equipped with services such as safe water, sanitation and electricity, so they can avoid contamination and store and prepare food safely. Houses of higher income groups are also likely to be in safer and healthier locations than the houses of the poor. Crowding and pollution devalues housing, so attracting the poor, while those who are better off can afford to live elsewhere, even commuting long distances, if necessary, so as to be able to live in safe and attractive places. People on higher incomes are also likely to be more educated than poorer people, which brings further benefits in terms of a better understanding of health issues as well as a greater capacity to act to improve their health.

At the national level, economic conditions determine the options available to governments for the level of investment in human development, including education and health care and the type and quality of care to provide. Health facilities are almost always better in rich countries than in poor countries, and there is greater investment in infrastructure to improve living conditions. Many contemporary developing countries are unable to provide all their people with access to health services. For example, in most of the 20 countries with the highest under-five mortality in 1994 less than 40 per cent of the population had access to safe water, less than 30 per cent had safe sanitation and less than 70 per cent had access to health services.[8] Where facilities are available they are likely to be poorly equipped. In 1996 it was reported that sterilizers were not available at 50–70 per cent of reproductive health centres in Ghana, Nigeria and Burkina Faso, even though they frequently carry out invasive procedures. Up to 50 per cent did not have blood pressure gauges, one of the most basic pieces of health monitoring equipment.[9]

The association between the agricultural resource endowment of a country, natural environmental conditions and health is no longer as direct as in the past. One aspect that remains is the regional distribution of some infectious diseases, which exposes populations living in the tropics to a range of serious illnesses which are not found in temperate climates, such as haemorrhagic fevers, filariasis and schistosomiasis. Even in the tropics the higher income groups are more able to protect themselves from infection, since many tropical diseases are carried by insects or other parasites, which can be avoided by living and working where exposure is less likely. Aside from this association of certain diseases with particular environments, health patterns are more likely to be related to economic than to environmental conditions. Although diets tend to be healthiest in countries which can produce a wide range of nutritious food, the capacity to grow abundant food does not necessarily ensure good population health, since cash crops may be produced rather than food. This can increase local food prices and contribute to poor diets. On the other hand, wealth derived from trade, minerals or technological innovation may offset the disadvantages of an unfavourable agricultural environment and harsh climate. For example, the extraordinary wealth of the oil-rich nations of the Middle East, such as the United Arab Emirates, compensates for the barren desert surroundings, enabling the privileged classes to live in air conditioned comfort with lavish consumption of imported goods.

Core–periphery relations have influenced the choice of health care model adopted by developing countries. Since the evolution of Western curative health care played an important part in the health transition in industrialized countries, it was widely assumed by colonial powers that this was the only suitable model of health care for developing countries. This attitude persisted well into the post Second World War period. It is indisputable that Western medicine has the capacity to provide excellent health care and has extremely advanced life saving capacities. Even so, it has performed poorly in some contemporary developing countries. Although it has brought enormous benefits to world health as a whole, actual gains in health and survival have often been well below potential health gains. The main reason for this is that the type of medicine provided is often inappropriate for local needs, not because of any intrinsic defects, but because it emphasized curative rather than preventive medicine, is too costly, too sophisticated and too remote from the people.

The spread of Western medicine into developing countries was spearheaded by the most costly element, hospital and clinic-based curative medicine, which depend on sophisticated equipment and medicines and a hierarchy of trained staff. A full Western medical qualification requires a substantial investment of at least seven years' training, so in many countries doctors are in short supply, and are more likely to be male than female. Where there is a shortage of doctors most of their time is inevitably taken up with curing the sick, and they have little time to advise on preventive medicine. They may also have little time or capacity to tailor services to particular cultural or social needs. Western trained doctors thus tend to be highly technical, predominantly male, reliant on sophisticated equipment and remote from their patients.

These features can lead to various problems. First, many countries cannot sustain the high costs of running sophisticated medical facilities. In such circumstances facilities are likely to become degraded with inadequate attention to hygiene and maintenance of sterile conditions and equipment, shortages of medication and reuse of items which are designed to be disposable, such as syringes and needles. In such circumstances health facilities may create almost as many problems by cross-infection and contamination as they cure.

Second, people living in traditional communities may feel alienated from Western medicine and fear or distrust it. There are many examples of culturally inappropriate health strategies. For example, where only male medical personnel are available, women may be reluctant to seek treatment.[10] In Indonesia young midwives were posted to remote communities where only older women were trusted to deliver babies,[11] and in Botswana women were brought from traditional communities to deliver their babies in frightening and unsympathetic modern hospitals.[12] In parts of Papua New Guinea, the hierarchical nature of medical training has led to wastage rather than efficiency where clients insist on being treated by the most highly trained practitioner and refuse services from less qualified staff. Trained doctors, who are in short supply, are thus unable to delegate even minor procedures, such as dressing small wounds.

Third, the importance in the health transition of simultaneous progress in environmental health is sometimes overlooked. The Western medical package is often accepted uncritically by health officials in developing countries, largely because the industrialized countries, who set international health policy and standards, also provide significant amounts of health assistance. The provision of safe water, sanitation and acceptable housing to entire populations is more likely to require substantial amounts of local investment. In resource poor countries with limited tax bases, it may be allocated low priority. Yet, as a Papua New Guinea doctor once remarked to one of the authors, unless his local city council makes the water supply safe, all his time spent on treating children with diarrhoea is nothing more than a 'band-aid' solution to the problem.

Within countries, health facilities are generally superior and more accessible in urban areas than in rural areas. Even if health services are free, rural dwellers may be unable to use them unless they are within easy reach, because they may not be able to afford the cost of travel or overnight accommodation. Sometimes it is impossible to access health services without payment of some kind, even where they are deemed to be available free of charge. Ugandan women queuing at a child health centre told one of the authors that their children would not receive treatment unless they gave the clinic sister a small gift, such as a bottle of soft drink, a few coins or some fruit or vegetables. Because of their privileged position these public officials expected payment, even though they were salaried staff employed to deliver free services. Queuing times at this Kampala clinic were often five or six hours, so it was very inconvenient for women who had long distances to travel or were caring for other small children, and many children did not complete immunization courses or return for growth monitoring.

Most countries have a dual health system, comprising both a public and a private health sector. Sometimes there may be a combination of modern and traditional medicine, and sometimes there may be both public and private modern medicine. Socialist countries have typically tried to achieve only a single, free public system based on modern medicine, but it is common to find private fee-for-service systems existing parallel to public systems, either covertly or overtly. In Vietnam, for example, doctors working in the public health system are poorly paid, so they accept private patients after clinic hours to boost their incomes. Recognizing that this is a way of expanding health services without further state investment, the Vietnamese government allows private practitioners to use public health facilities to treat private patients. Since the Vietnamese public health system is resource-poor, access to services is limited by long waiting times. Those patients who can afford to pay for treatment can thus avoid queues and obtain immediate treatment.[13] The downside of this system is that, since doctors prefer to treat patients who pay them directly, it has contributed to poorer service in the public sector, hence further disadvantaging the poor. Moreover, it has proved difficult to regulate private practitioners since there is a strong suppliers' market.

A stark example at the international level of how disease avoidance strategies practised by the rich can disadvantage the poor is the case of malaria prophylaxis. Since the 1990s an expensive medication, mefloquine hydroxide (sold as Lariam), which was formerly reserved only for treatment of severe attacks of malaria, has been taken as a prophylactic by Americans and some other Europeans visiting malarial areas. As a consequence some strains of malaria are developing a resistance to mefloquine and it has become less effective as a treatment. This has left local populations in malarial areas with fewer strategies for treating this potentially fatal illness.

The adoption of primary health care strategies since the 1970s has proved a more cost-effective approach to improving health. Although primary health care is a complement rather than a substitute for curative medicine, by promoting health rather than treating illness it is more able to foster good health as defined by the WHO.[14] Primary health care is based on the equitable treatment of all members of society, community involvement and intersectoral coordination. The last of these is necessary to ensure improvements to create a healthy environment, such as establishing a water supply, which are likely to be beyond the scope and resources of the health sector.

The basic principles of primary health care are that there should be education in methods of preventing illness, promotion of healthy nutrition, availability of safe water and sanitation, access to maternal and child health and family planning services, immunization against major infectious diseases, prevention and control of local endemic diseases, appropriate treatment of common diseases and injuries, and provision of essential medication.[15] Many primary health care strategies can be implemented at relatively low cost compared with curative medicine, yet can achieve substantial improvements in health by stemming illness at its source rather than tackling it after it has developed. One of the most effective contributions of Western medical technology to mortality reduction in contemporary developing countries has been the Expanded Program on Immunization, a primary health care initiative to protect children from some of the major causes of child death. Another cheap but powerful primary health care contribution has been the simple and obvious strategy of providing health education for individuals and communities.

Primary health care can be seen as a 'bottom-up' approach to health care, while curative based health strategies imply a 'top-down' approach. The choice of approach to health care is thus analogous to the approaches to economic development discussed in Chapter 2.

SOCIOLOGICAL DETERMINANTS OF HEALTH

Whereas external factors determine the available health options, the health choices made by individuals are shaped by a complex web of cultural values, attitudes and behaviours. The underlying sociological determinants relate to the culture and customs of the society in which the individual lives. Cultural values influence the way individuals perceive the world and their place within it. Central to all cultures are specific norms regarding social organization. Those which affect health include the roles ascribed to men and women; gender equity or inequity; the expectation of parents as regards their children; attitudes to sexuality; taboos and social constraints; and prescriptions for appropriate behaviour.

Health research shows consistent associations between socio-cultural factors and health. For example, the status of women has a direct bearing not only on their own health but also on the health of their children. Women with higher status, particularly educated women, are more able to ensure good nutrition for their children and themselves, more likely to recognize illness in their children, and more likely to take action to treat it.[16] Parents who expect their daughters to enter the labour force are more likely to invest in their nutrition, health and education than are parents who expect their daughters to marry and leave home at a young age, thus returning little or no benefit to the family.[17]

Culture also affects health through customs relating to its more material aspects, such as living arrangements, type of housing, work patterns, dietary preferences and dress. For example, crowded living arrangements with poorly ventilated spaces can increase disease transmission; diets high in animal fats contribute to high rates of cardiovascular disease; and restrictive clothing, coupled with social expectations that movement should be slow and dignified, can lead to lack of physical fitness.

The poorest countries, where living standards are lowest and there is a high prevalence of infectious disease, are often very conservative and allow little scope for individual variation in lifestyles because conformity is valued. Although some wealthy countries such as the oil states also have very conservative cultures, the poverty of many people in conservative societies further restricts their lifestyle options. In such societies those in the lower social strata tend to be the most conservative because they can win respect by reaffirming important cultural norms. In contrast, those belonging to the higher social strata, who are likely to be wealthier, are often the first to experiment with new lifestyles, not only because they have more opportunity but also because their high status protects them from criticism for non-conformity.

Modern, industrialized societies are generally more accepting of non-conformity, so they allow more scope for individual variation in lifestyles, for both high and low social strata and high and low income groups. Although living conditions are generally better because of higher incomes and greater investment in infrastructure and health services, there is more opportunity to choose unhealthy lifestyle habits, which can contribute to early-onset NCDs. In modernized countries most food is purchased from retail outlets, many jobs are sedentary, and alcohol and cigarettes are usually freely available. Moreover, because of price structures in the food industry, and because physical exercise requires effort while drinking alcohol, smoking and eating induce a relaxed and congenial state, unhealthy behaviour tends to be cheaper, easier and, on the surface at least, more attractive than healthy behaviour. In such circumstances, where a wide range of lifestyle choices are available, the pursuit of healthy behaviour is likely to require strong motivation and will power.

In modern societies some people practise healthy behaviour for reasons that are unrelated to their perceptions of health, because it is their preferred behaviour or because of their work, income or place of residence. Other possible motivations to pursue a healthy lifestyle might be social, such as to present a healthy and more attractive image to other people, or personal, such as the satisfaction and feeling of well-being that comes from fitness and health, or an understanding of the causes of NCDs. Always, however, sustained effort over time and continual decisions to choose healthy rather than unhealthy behavioural options are required. This means that whenever factors intervene to undermine personal objectives and will-power, people are likely to opt for the easier choice.

CULTURAL PERCEPTIONS OF HEALTH AND BODY IMAGE

Perceptions of health and the ability of individuals to influence it vary markedly between cultures. Several theories have been developed to explain health-related behaviour. The Health Belief Model[18] argues that health-related behaviour is determined according to individual evaluations of an outcome, and the expectation that a specific behaviour will produce that outcome. Attribution theory suggests that the way people attribute causation affects their beliefs about illness, which, in turn, determines their health behaviour.[19] In terms of attribution theory, those who have an external 'locus of control' believe illness is caused by external forces over which they have little or no control, while those who have an internal 'locus of control' believe that their actions can influence health outcomes.[20]

Studies in many countries have shown that more traditional societies generally have an external locus of control, but with education this changes towards an internal locus of control. Those with an external locus of control commonly attribute illness to factors such as witchcraft, or certain behaviours and foods which have no scientifically proven connection with illness. Among the more traditional peoples of West Aceh, Indonesia, for example, disease is thought to have three main causes: being touched by ghosts or evil spirits; black magic; and a group of factors including bad weather, dust and dirt, heat and eating particular foods.[21]

Health-related behaviour is also affected by perceptions of beauty, body image and appropriate behaviour. In the most modernized societies the ideal for both men and women is a lean, muscular body. In other countries a certain amount of body fat is considered more attractive, or more appropriate for people of a particular age. For example, traditional values in the Pacific associate obesity with high status.[22] While young people are admired for being slender and muscular, and these characteristics are also acceptable in adults, so are heavy bodies.[23] Moreover, adults are expected to behave with dignity and decorum. This means slow movement and modest clothing. Activities such as running around in sports clothing are acceptable in children, but are considered inappropriate for adults, especially mature women. As more people are exposed to Western television and film their perceptions of body image and behaviour are being modified to some extent. Even so, as will be shown in our interview data in Chapter 9, many people enjoy such entertainment but still maintain their own perceptions of what is appropriate for themselves and their society.

Individuals in many societies do not necessarily perceive a direct association between eating habits, weight gain and NCDs. Even what might seem to be the most obvious connection, such as between body weight and quantity of food consumed, may not be recognized. The cause of this is actually far more complex than a lack of basic education, and must take into account deep-rooted beliefs related to religion, spirituality and perceptions of life which may be quite alien to mainstream Western viewpoints. Even in modern contexts it may be difficult to convince people that eating certain foods will make them fat when it does not happen instantly, and when not all people are affected in the same way. Young teenagers, for example, tend to be more active and have a greater requirement for proteins and fats than adults, and so may be able to consume large quantities of calorie-rich food without gaining excess weight. When their metabolism slows as they mature, the cause of any weight gain may not be recognized, and it may not be appreciated that they should abandon eating habits which did not lead to weight gain in the past.

Another factor affecting eating patterns is that food performs an important social function in virtually all cultures. On a day-to-day level, food sharing is an important social activity in both developed and developing countries. Eating together bonds families and friendships, is a fundamental part of hospitality and also, at times, a demonstration of wealth and prestige. In both developed and developing countries alcohol consumption may be considered a normal part of social life and hospitality, except where it is specifically excluded by religious or other beliefs. People engaged in traditional subsistence activities tend to expend enough energy to prevent very substantial weight gain, even if they are consuming nutritious diets such as the Pacific diet of starchy staples, fish, fruit and coconut. However, when modern sedentary lifestyles replace subsistence activities, such diets can readily lead to obesity, especially if supplemented by modern convenience foods and alcohol. In many countries the expenditure of energy for subsistence has decreased dramatically for those employed in white collar work, while the social importance of food and drink has been preserved. Unless they eat and drink frugally or take exercise people are at risk of becoming overweight.

PERCEPTIONS OF RISK AND STRESS

One of the most important factors that prevents people from making the effort to follow a healthy lifestyle is individual perception of health risks. Even when they understand the health consequences of some behaviours, they may assess their personal risk as low. For example, many people in Australia and other developed countries still smoke, even though cigarette packets carry very blunt health warnings, such as 'Smoking causes lung cancer' and 'Smoking kills'.

One reason for underestimation of personal risk is that NCDs such as cancer, heart disease and diabetes, tend to take many years to develop, and even then do not affect everyone who is at risk. Hence, the connection between unhealthy behaviour and disease is not very direct. It has been estimated that every cigarette smoked reduces life expectancy at age 20 by 7 minutes, while people who consume five or more alcoholic drinks per day reduce their life expectancy at age 20 years by at least 30 minutes per day.[24] Yet nearly everyone knows of people who smoked and drank heavily all their lives and still lived to be 80 or 90 years old.

Most smokers indulge for many years before they develop lung cancer, and some smokers never do. Similarly, the consumption of large amounts of alcohol, and a diet too rich in fats and sugars does not have an instantaneous impact on health. There are numerous examples of people who have been substantially overweight for many years but appear to be otherwise healthy. There is not necessarily any outward sign that their heart is under strain and is more likely to fail before they reach an advanced age than if they were not overweight. There are also people who appear to be very fit and not overweight but who collapse and die of a heart attack while taking vigorous exercise or even when resting.

This does not mean that the statistics are incorrect; rather, they refer to average risk and not to any definite outcome. Being slim and fit means a much lower risk of heart attack, but it does not mean no risk at all. Being obese means a greatly increased risk of heart attack, but is not a guarantee that one will occur. As a consequence people are able to excuse their own poor health habits by persuading themselves that they will be one of the lucky ones. We can conjecture that it would be a very different scenario if the connection between unhealthy behaviour and disease were more direct, such as if all smokers developed lung cancer one week after they smoked their first packet of cigarettes. Since this is not so, it can be difficult to use risk arguments to persuade people to abandon activities which give them pleasure or which would require a great effort to give up.

Stress is widespread among workers in modern developed economies, as a consequence of the fast pace of life and the excessive demands of their jobs. Urbanization is a leading cause of increased stress, and studies have shown that stress arising from day-to-day difficulties may produce more illness than even major life events such as bereavement.[25] Those who are marginalized by modern economies and forced into inactivity may also experience stress. In developing countries there can be the additional stress-related factor of having to cope with significant socioeconomic change and possible tension in relation to issues of personal identity and competing cultural values.

Although some degree of stress may provide stimulation and have a beneficial effect on health, excessive stress or that which occurs frequently over a long period of time can lead to illness. Stress affects health both directly and indirectly. On the one hand, stress increases anxiety and vulnerability to illness which are risk factors for disorders of the cardiovascular system, the digestive system, the respiratory system and the skin.[26] On the other hand, stressed people are more likely to engage in behaviours which increase health risks, such as overeating, smoking and drinking excessive quantities of alcohol. These behaviours can be linked to aggressive advertising strategies which promote cigarettes and alcohol as fashionable mechanisms for stress relief. Cigarette smoking is a form of addictive behaviour which is used universally as a way of relieving stress.[27] People who have no ready outlet for stress-induced feelings often choose to smoke as well as to overeat and drink too much alcohol as outlets for feelings of frustration. Others, especially young people, may adopt these behaviours because they are seeking new and stimulating sensations to relieve boredom.[28] Less regulation of advertising in developing countries means that such products are likely to be distributed without the health warnings manufacturers are obliged to display in more developed countries.

Modern, industrialized societies tend to offer more opportunities for stress relief than conservative, traditional societies. Sporting facilities are generally more available, it is usually acceptable for both men and women of all ages to take vigorous exercise and there is more anonymity so people tend to feel less constrained in what they do. Paradoxically, taking exercise is often perceived as impractical because it requires too much effort or too much time compared with less healthy ways of relieving stress.[29] It may be more difficult to relieve stress where tradition is strong, especially in small communities. Attempts to externalize feelings, such as by expressing anger, or uninhibited behaviour are more likely to lead to social conflict or criticism. However, the repression and internalization of anger increase personal stress. The increase in pulse rate and blood pressure in people who repress their anger can be up to three times as great as in people who externalize it with aggressive behaviour.[30] Hence, those who appear to be passive may be increasing their risk of degenerative disease even more than those who become aggressive.

STDs, A SPECIAL CASE

Before concluding this discussion of the determinants of health, mention must be made of sexually transmitted diseases (STDs), which constitute a special category of infectious disease because of their social connotations and the difficulty of treating them. To date, modern medical technology has been noticeably less effective in controlling STDs than most other infectious diseases. Some STDs, such as syphilis and gonorrhoea have been known for a long time, but although antibiotics appeared to offer an effective cure and although STDs can only be transmitted by infected people, they remain a significant health problem.

One reason for the persistence of STDs is that because of the stigma associated with contracting them, and because the symptoms are not always obvious, those who are infected often do not seek treatment until they have already infected others. Another problem is that STDs are often extremely difficult to treat. Syphilis is virtually incurable unless treated in its early stages, and at the time of writing herpes simplex and *chlamydia* are widely regarded as intractable and difficult to treat. As yet there is no vaccine and no effective treatment for HIV/AIDS, which has reached epidemic proportions in some countries, and appears to be fatal in most cases.

Although most STDs can be prevented by using condoms, use remains very low in most countries. In 1994 it was estimated that only 5 per cent of couples worldwide were using condoms, and only 3 per cent in less developed regions.[31] This is primarily because of culturally determined attitudes, including the unacceptability of condoms themselves, reluctance to plan for or disturb sexual intimacy, embarrassment associated with obtaining condoms, fear of social condemnation of illicit sexual activity and factors which limit the ability of women to protect their own health.[32] This has led to a sustained and possibly increasing prevalence of STDs in both traditional and modernized societies. The transmission of STDs is also accelerated by some traditional perceptions of the cause of illness and by individual perceptions of risk.

To successfully control STDs it is necessary for societies to make it acceptable to discuss their most intimate and private acts, not only socially sanctioned conjugal sex but also illicit and extra-nuptial sexual activity. It is also necessary to persuade individuals to modify their private sexual behaviour and, if they become infected, to put aside their inhibitions and seek treatment for conditions which they may find acutely embarrassing. In view of this it is hardly surprising that STDs remain a significant health problem in most countries.

The case of STDs dramatically illustrates the importance of sociological factors as determinants of health and health risks. Although external factors determine exposure to the risk of illness, sociological factors determine the lifestyle choices that increase or diminish that risk. Both external and sociological factors are, in turn, determined to a large extent by global economic forces. Whether an individual lives in a core or a peripheral state, their position in the social hierarchy and their earning capacity all impact on their health. An understanding of both groups of these and their interrelationships is essential for the study of health patterns in any country, and for the formulation of effective health policy.

The following chapters look at three case studies, taking the pattern of disease as an indicator of the impact of modernization on societal health. Two are drawn from the former Soviet Union's sphere of influence, and illustrate the difficulties faced in the transition from a centrally planned to a market economic system. In these countries the main influences on health are external, related to economic and environmental changes which have been determined largely by contact with the former Soviet Union. The third case study illustrates the vast reach of global forces. Greater attention is paid to the Marshall Islands because the factors influencing health are more complex, and are both external and sociological. There is uneven progress in health and a high prevalence of early-onset NCDs, despite an apparently favourable environment and high levels of economic assistance from the USA. Although its location is remote and its resource base limited, the Marshall Islands offers the option of a healthy lifestyle. Many Marshallese, however, do not have one.

The three states in the case studies have different histories and their own social, economic and geographical characteristics. Their common experience is exposure to global economic forces which increasingly determine the options and choices available to their governments and their populations. The process of modernization, and subsequent marginalization of various groups and individuals, has had direct effects on their patterns of health. The states formerly dominated by, or part of, the Soviet Union are facing the particular difficulty of the disrupting effects of transition to radically different political and economic systems. The Marshall Islands is also profoundly influenced by its relationship with the USA. All three states, like the majority of the world's states, are enmeshed in economic transactions which have a tendency to emphasize divisions in wealth and to impact on health.

Chapter 4

The Process of Marginalization

Marginalization is a process which may span many years. Although an individual may become marginalized by a single event such as loss of employment, at the state level the process is normally a consequence of a gradual erosion of economic autonomy. Forces of interaction and domination between individuals and communities shift and evolve over time. For centuries this was largely a consequence of territorial expansion and retreat. The great empires of Greece and Rome expanded into new areas and exploited them in order to support the great civilizations at their core. In the 17th century, the Spanish and Portuguese expanded into South America in a similar way and, subsequently, with other European colonial powers, extended into Asia, Africa and the Pacific.

For the most part the colonial powers exported raw materials from their colonies to support activities at the core of their empires. In the 18th and 19th centuries such economic colonialism provided essential raw materials to support the expansion of the Industrial Revolution in Europe. In most cases the processing of raw materials took place in the core countries, leaving the colonies little opportunity to develop their own industrial base. Even so, a large proportion of the goods manufactured in the core countries were re-exported to the colonies where they were sold for a profit as they were now more valuable than the raw materials.

Parallel to the core–peripheral relationship between the colonial power and its territories were core–peripheral relationships between groups within states. Despite overall economic growth, some groups and individuals were disadvantaged relative to others and failed to reap the benefits of this growth. In the case of the UK, huge disparities developed in the conditions experienced by the ruling elite and the workers. Health conditions in early industrial cities were appalling for the poor. Although in recent times years of welfare state interventions have endeavoured to ensure that the basic needs of all British citizens are met, these historical distinctions have persisted and the poor are still marginalized. This pattern is replicated in the USA and other developed states.

Each of these empires had periods of expansion and contraction. Most were based on the physical occupation of their colonial territories, which was costly and difficult to maintain in the face of rebellion. In the case of the Roman Empire it is argued that the difficulty of maintaining such a vast and far-reaching territory was a major contributing factor to the decline of the Empire. In the post Second World War period there was a general move towards decolonization, when most of the European powers physically withdrew their colonial administrative structures from the territories. However, the well-established economic relationships tended to continue, including the export of raw materials from former colonial territories to core countries, and the export of manufactured consumer goods from core countries to their former territories. In this way the underlying power relationship continued in the form of a trade partnership.

Russia, Japan and the USA joined the group of colonial powers relatively late in the colonial era, but built some of the biggest spheres of influence. The defeat of Japan in the Second World War caused its empire to be dismantled, but the Russian Empire, as the USSR, and the USA sphere of influence, which was never formally acknowledged as a colonial empire, survived into the post-war period. By remaining a pseudo-colonial power, the USA was in a better position to develop the type of economic relationships that developed in the post-war period, which were easier to maintain and more enduring.

In the contemporary world geographical location is less important in core–periphery relationships. Electronic credit transfer and investments occur almost instantaneously around the globe, yet there remain identifiable centres of international finance. London, New York and Tokyo are examples of major centres of financial activity, although many of the financial transactions they service no longer represent territorially based interests. As a consequence of the increased scale of activity of multinational corporations, foreign direct investment is almost wholly associated with the accumulation of capital as opposed to broader foreign and domestic policy.

The effect of improved communications in reducing the importance of geographical location has modified and strengthened core–periphery links.

Divisions in access to resources, wealth and opportunity for advancement increase the degree to which individuals and communities are becoming marginalized from the benefits of current trends in development. To be 'marginal' now has greater consequences than might have been the case in the past. As a greater number of structures and processes develop international or global dimensions the consequences of where individuals and communities rank in a range of hierarchies have additional implications. An important impact of marginalization is on health. Although health conditions were not necessarily better in core than in peripheral countries during the colonial period, and in early industrial cities were almost certainly substantially worse, core–periphery relationships have long influenced the standard of facilities and health care.

For many developing states, geographical factors such as remoteness and transport costs remain important. Of greater significance are economic developments, aided by technological innovations, which have led to growing disparities of wealth and a continuing reinforcement of the dominance of the core states over those on the periphery. Post-Cold War political re-orientating has also played a role in this process. Clearly some states which were more reliant on superpower investment than others have had to make greater adjustments.

This chapter examines the origins of marginality in our three case studies, to demonstrate the mechanisms which lead to marginalization relative to global powers. Their experiences are representative of the experiences of many contemporary states outside the core areas. It describes their historical relations with their neighbours and the role thrust upon them as a result of superpower rivalry, and shows how this has led to marginalization not only in economic terms but also in health and well-being.

MONGOLIA

Mongolia is landlocked between two major powers with histories of imperialism, Russia and China. Although roughly half the size of India with a total land area of 605,000 square miles (1.6 million square kilometres), its population is only a little over 2 million. It has a severe semi-arid continental climate with average temperatures below freezing for six months of the year. Despite its wealth of rich grasslands during the summer months, it is a harsh environment which has required its population to develop special survival skills.

Mongolia's current status is far removed from its history as a hegemonic Asian power. At one time it was the core of a far-reaching empire. The Mongolian people comprise more than a hundred nomadic tribes, which ranged widely across territories now subdivided into the Mongolian People's Republic, North and Western China and Eastern Russia. Chingis Khan unified the Mongolian tribes and founded the Mongol Empire in 1206. At its zenith it extended over most of modern-day China and Korea and reached as far as Poland. The vast extent of this territory eventually exceeded the capacity of the Mongolian Khans to govern it, and a period of civil strife and rebellion led to the gradual disintegration of the Empire during the 14th and 15th centuries and its subsequent absorption as a territory of the Manchurian Empire.

As pastoralists the Mongolian people depended on their herds of cattle, horses, goats, sheep and camels for all their needs. Land was not owned by individuals, but wealth was measured by the number of livestock owned. The imposition of boundaries by the Manchu rulers in 1691 was much resented. The Manchus divided the Mongolian heartland into Inner Mongolia, which became a province of China, and Northern (Outer) Mongolia, which eventually became the Socialist People's Republic of Mongolia. Northern Mongolia remained under Manchu domination. Increasing Chinese pressure on Mongolians, in particular the imposition of restrictions on the spread of Russian and Japanese influences and Mongolian access to investment capital, provoked the rebellion of 1911 and the Mongolian declaration of independence from the Manchu Dynasty.[1]

Although China itself was to establish its own republic the following year, it was not ready to give up Northern Mongolia. For the next decade the Mongolian independence movement struggled to achieve recognition and autonomy. In an effort to achieve this end it actively sought the assistance of Russia, its other colonial neighbour, and used Russian weapons in its independence struggles.[2] The emergence of strong leadership in 1921 finally brought a second, successful revolution, and led to the founding of the Socialist People's Republic of Mongolia in 1924. However, from the very beginning it had a close and dependent relationship with the USSR as a satellite state.

The 1921 revolutionary movement had been infused with Marxist-Leninist ideology, and the formation of the Mongolian Communist Party was an integral part of the process of independence. This communist orientation led naturally to the adoption of a planned economy largely based on the Soviet model.[3] Thus, the threat of encroachment from the Chinese Empire led Mongolia to accept Soviet influences and investment and place itself within the sphere of influence of a different superpower.

Japanese expansion in the 1930s enhanced the strategic importance of Mongolia to the USSR as a buffer state. Russia forged strong military links with Mongolia to protect it from Japanese invasion, and improved communications, including doubling the track of the trans-Siberian railway. In the 1920s an initially disastrous programme to collectivize Mongolian livestock herds was introduced. Vast numbers of animals died when the traditional form of livestock herding was disrupted by the imposition of the Soviet model of primary production. In 1933 the first factory was opened, which gave the population a new opportunity to abandon the traditional lifestyle.[4]

Increasing conflict in China and Mongolia's perception of ever greater threats from Far Eastern expansion during the Second World War and early post-war years facilitated the growth of Soviet influence. In the 1950s and 1960s, however, Chinese overtures increased in an effort to woo Mongolia away from the Soviet influence into the Chinese sphere of influence. In 1960 Chou En-Lai offered Mongolia a steel mill and a 300,000-man labour force but, after consultation with Russia, Mongolia refused the offer and instead accepted Russian development of a smaller steel mill on the same site.[5]

Both Sino-Soviet and Sino-Mongolian relationships subsequently deteriorated in the 1960s and 1970s, while Russian investment in Mongolia increased. This culminated in the development of the Erdenet copper and molybdenum mining operation in the 1970s. This massive operation, one of the ten largest copper mines in the world, intensified Mongolia's symbiotic relationship with the USSR, but also emphasized the core–periphery nature of this relationship. The produce from Erdenet was exported as raw material to feed Soviet processing plants and supply Soviet markets. By 1979 it was apparent that:

> *Once a pivotal area in world geopolitics for close to two*
> *thousand years, Mongolia is now a pawn in a great*
> *power competition... Modern Mongolians reject the*
> *proposition that Mongolia is Chinese territory, but they*
> *are also distressed to think that their people are a client-*
> *state of Russia.*[6]

Although Mongolia benefited from Soviet technology and Soviet education and was able to use this as the basis for its own modernization, it remained marginalized on the edge of the Soviet sphere of influence and its development was not comparable with that at the core.

The Mongolian–Soviet relationship, as with any imperial or colonial model, thus involved the development of an economic structure based on the flow of wealth from the periphery to the core. There was no basis for socioeconomic equity when the Soviet Empire collapsed in 1989 and Mongolia was forced to make a rapid transition to a market economy. The loss of Soviet investment has resulted in declining per capita incomes, a higher prevalence of lifestyle-related disease and an overall reduction in welfare expenditure.[7] In this instance the negative impacts of being a peripheral state were exacerbated by the dramatic nature of the socioeconomic transition.

UZBEKISTAN

As the largest of the former Soviet Republics, Uzbekistan is roughly the size of Sweden with a land area of 174,000 square miles (450,000 square kilometres). It has a population of about 21 million. It is situated in the semi-arid Central Asian region; almost three-fifths of the country is desert and steppe and the remainder comprises fertile valleys in the foothills of high mountain ranges.

The Uzbek people have inhabited their current territory for centuries, and at one time they were part of the Mongolian Empire. Following the withdrawal of the Mongols, Tamerlane conquered and annexed a territory in Central Asia stretching from Turkey to Iran to India. In 1369 he proclaimed Samarkand his capital, and it became one of the great influential centres of Islam.[8] The Uzbek region prospered as a centre of Muslim culture, trade and commerce until 1865 when Russian troops conquered Tashkent and proclaimed it the administrative centre of the newly founded Russian Turkestan.

The Turkestan Soviet Socialist Republic (SSR) was created after the 1917 Communist Revolution. This fusing of ethnic groups was ambitious and had potential for serious conflict. Accordingly, in 1924 the Turkestan SSR was divided into five separate republics, one of which was the Uzbek SSR.[9] Although initially the Russian Tsars may have been attracted to Uzbekistan for its mineral resources, including gold, copper, lead, zinc and tungsten, they soon adapted its rich soils and, at that time, abundant water resources to cotton cultivation.[10] Cotton cultivation expanded and became more intensive when it was collectivized after 1917.

The Uzbek people protested against the destruction of traditional land tenure systems and the reduced availability of food crops following the establishment of a near monoculture of cotton on collective farms. Cotton radically altered existing socioeconomic patterns, with a subsequent impact on lifestyles and health. Collectives utilized intensive farming techniques, and became increasingly reliant on mechanization and the intensive utilization of fertilizer and pesticides. While this agricultural modernization on the Uzbek periphery had negative local consequences, the benefits generally accrued to those at the core of first the Tsarist, and later the Soviet Empires.

Like Mongolia, Uzbekistan faced massive economic shock when the USSR disintegrated; it became independent in 1991 and is currently experiencing the downside of political and economic independence. Societal and economic impacts within Uzbekistan were widespread, not least the loss of more than 19 per cent of its GDP which had been received as aid transfers from the Soviet Union.[11] These effects were compounded by the negative growth that had been experienced in most sectors of the economy throughout the 1980s. The consequences of environmentally destructive policies were also becoming apparent, notably in the Aral Sea region. The water area of the Aral Sea has been progressively reducing in recent years because water from its two major feeder rivers, the Amudarya and the Syrdarya were diverted into irrigation. The long-term effect has been a massive retreat of the Aral Sea shoreline by 60–80 kilometres, and loss of water in the Aral region. An additional problem has been contamination from toxic chemicals that had drained into the sea in the past, not only polluting the water but also becoming air-borne as the seabed was exposed to the action of winds. Climatic conditions in the affected areas are such that this dispersal has covered hundreds of square miles.

The Aral Sea example illustrates a number of points. First it shows how crucial the disposal of waste products can be in terms of the health of the ecosystem and highlights the requirement for sustainable development policies. It also demonstrates how, like many other emerging states around the world, Uzbekistan has had to cope with a colonial legacy of the long-term consequences of previously exploitative practices that failed to consider the future health of local populations. Aspects of political control and the consequence of a wholly economic growth-driven policy orientation are brought into question.

The spiral of decline in evidence in those parts of Uzbekistan most affected by the Aral Sea crisis emphasizes disparities of wealth created by core–periphery relations. This is a process of negative reinforcement. Just as the principle of comparative advantage consistently strengthens the structure of existing power relationships, once a process of decline has begun, it is difficult to reverse. The Commonwealth of Independent States has now pledged to attempt a revitalization of the Aral Sea region, but this requires investment at a time of national financial constraints. Having greater local autonomy can be seen as an improvement for the former Soviet Republics. Yet, they remain in a marginalized position due to the economic structure they have inherited and the lack of capital investment available to make good the mistakes of the past.

Even so, breaking away from a colonial relationship does not immediately bring social and economic benefits. Depending on the level of local involvement of the metropolitan power, a sudden withdrawal of support can be catastrophic. Many Uzbeks and Mongolians, especially those in low income groups, would argue that they were better off before the Soviet collapse and the achievement of independence because they were more able to meet their basic needs. In the case of Uzbekistan there was a heavy reliance on Soviet economic support for health care. The newly independent state thus faced stark choices in terms of where to invest its limited funds. As with most states, the emphasis has been placed on promoting economic growth as opposed to meeting basic welfare needs. Again this reinforces marginalization within the state, as those in greatest need are likely to suffer the harshest consequences of cuts in government spending.

Marginalization in the former Soviet Union has operated at several levels. In geographic terms, relative distance from Moscow has been important. As such, Mongolia was further removed from the decision-making process than Uzbekistan, not only because of its remoteness but also because by remaining outside the USSR it did not have representation on the Supreme Soviet. Within each Republic there were socioeconomic divisions based on levels of involvement with the Communist Party and resulting patronage. Such divisions continue, but are now based more on economic rather than party political grounds. Moreover, the evolution of global market forces has meant that the economic aspect of international relations has taken on greater importance. Economies in transition throughout Central Asia and Eastern Europe have particular difficulties in replacing the welfare provisions that existed, albeit in limited measures, under the Soviet system. Growing disparities of wealth, which appear in all of these economies, add to this problem.

Of equal importance to both Mongolia and Uzbekistan, as well as numerous other vulnerable economies and societies, is the historical development of a global political economy. The post-Second World War creation of what became known as the Bretton Woods system of international economic management has been as important as developments within their own regions. Even something as profound as the collapse of a neighbouring superpower has to be set within the broader context of global economic structures and processes.

One of the key elements of modernization and globalization has been that even the remotest and most isolated states are increasingly affected by events occurring well beyond their borders. Those states that came under the influence of the Soviet planned economic system felt the impact of Russia's relationship with the West. In part this can be linked to military expenditure resulting from superpower rivalry. Some analysts have gone so far as to suggest a causal connection between Soviet military spending and subsequent political disintegration. Regardless of the cause of this imperial collapse, it has had major implications for the Soviet satellite states in that they now have to survive in an already well-established global economic system. Crucially this is a system that has evolved with a particular set of values and power relationships.

In moving from the planned Soviet model to free market economics, Mongolia, Uzbekistan and other peripheral states are attempting to develop their economies from a fundamentally disadvantaged position. Under such circumstances it has already become apparent that there is significant social change taking place, with resulting disparities of wealth and well-being emerging as reflected in other societies adopting free market policies.

Thus, contemporary Mongolia and Uzbekistan have been shaped by their experience of domination and distorted development by the Soviet superpower, which has led to subsequent difficulties in coping with the transition to a free-market economy and the negative impacts on health of economic and social change. Our third case study, the Republic of the Marshall Islands, demonstrates that historical and political core–periphery relationships with the US superpower have led to similar economic difficulties and have had similar negative impacts on health, despite different political philosophies and the absence of an exploitable mineral or agricultural base. The following section traces the historical evolution of this pattern of domination and dependence.

REPUBLIC OF THE MARSHALL ISLANDS

The Marshall Islands was never the seat of a great empire, and became a focus of world attention only briefly during the 1940s and 1950s because of its strategic position in the Pacific. The experience of external contact with the outside world, the period as a United Nations Trust Territory and ongoing relations with the USA all shape the contemporary situation in the Marshall Islands. The model of a core–periphery relationship has increasing relevance to growing disparities of health, wealth and well-being; and to those that benefit from and those that are marginalized within the processes of modernization and globalization.

The Marshall Islands comprise 29 coral atolls and five small islands scattered across 750,000 square miles of the north-eastern Pacific Ocean (1.94 million square kilometres). The total land area is estimated at only about 70 square miles (181 square kilometres), and the mean height above sea level only 7 feet (2 metres). The thin coral soils are generally poor and unsuited to intensive cultivation. The main crops are coconut and breadfruit, while the sea provides abundant fish. The population has expanded rapidly since the 1960s and is currently estimated at between 56,000 and 60,000. Increasingly, traditional subsistence lifestyles are being abandoned in favour of migration to the two main urban areas of Majuro and Ebeye. Approximately 70 per cent of the total population now resides in these two centres.

Factors such as the limited resource base, distance from markets, climatic conditions and dependence on overseas aid has led to a situation of economic vulnerability for the Marshall Islands.[12] In addition to geographic and demographic factors the Marshall Islands' current situation has evolved as a result of a succession of colonial relationships.

Colonial contact in the Micronesian area as a whole has been a varied experience for the indigenous people. Dating from the initial Spanish explorations of the 16th century these first contacts were intermittent and restricted to relatively small areas, mainly in the Northern Marianas. It was not until the latter part of the 18th century that German settlement and the development of mining and plantations significantly altered traditional patterns of life. This trend was further exacerbated under Japanese influence and, most recently, that of the USA. There is an intriguingly ambiguous saying in the islands that summarises these contacts without specifying the intended meaning of the last word: 'The Spanish came for God, the Germans for Gold, the Japanese for Glory and the Americans for Good'.[13]

After the first period of European discovery, and before the German period of colonization, Micronesians had predominantly negative experiences from a range of transitory foreigners:

> *It was the ill-fortune of the Pacific Islanders that the exploiters who descended on them in the wake of the explorers were particularly predatory and undisciplined. Predatory because they all wanted to take something away – the fur of seals, the baleen of whales, the wood of the rainforests or the oil of the coconuts – and give nothing in return; undisciplined because most of them worked for themselves, and were unshackled by the restraints of government or company. There was no one to curb their excesses.*[14]

To say that nothing was given in return fails to take into account an array of lasting impacts on the islands. In parts of Micronesia these early contacts were responsible for the introduction of a range of infectious diseases and species that were to subsequently displace indigenous flora and fauna.[15] Technological advances that came via these early contacts were outweighed by life-threatening illness and resource depletion. Micronesians were forced to deal with this situation as best as they could.

Compared with the unrestricted excesses of the early exploiters a more established colonial presence had relative advantages for Micronesians. As the lesser of two evils it brought some improvements. For example under German rule:

> *the German administration succeeded in imposing its control throughout the islands of Micronesia without unduly antagonising the indigenous population. The Germans improved the territory considerably. They built roads, improved health care and sanitation, and explored the islands scientifically for economic potential. To a certain degree they protected the indigenous people from unscrupulous traders, and in general they attempted to ease them into contact with the Western world.[16]*

By far the most influential aspect of recent Marshallese history has been the impact of the Second World War and the subsequent status as a United Nations Strategic Trust Territory under the administering authority of the USA. The Japanese held control of the islands under a League of Nations Mandate following the First World War. As part of the Japanese East Asia Co-Prosperity Sphere, the Marshall Islands economy was boosted by capital investment, infrastructure development and Japanese technical expertise. The vast majority of the increase in wealth was exported to advance the Japanese economy, and in the latter part of Japanese rule the necessities of financing their war effort had a negative impact on the island territories.

There are numerous accounts of what amounted to slave labour in Japanese-controlled mining operations.[17] On at least one occasion, on Mili Atoll, the Marshallese took up arms against the Japanese. The leaders of this revolt were subsequently executed. There was also a higher level of exploitation without reinvestment. In economic terms the Japanese period can be viewed in a positive light in comparison with the relative neglect of Micronesian development under Trusteeship. The greatest failing of this period was the lack of integration of the Marshallese into key areas of decision-making.

As with the vast majority of colonial experiences the Japanese/Marshallese relationship has been characterized by exploitation. Despite the undoubted suffering experienced by the Marshall Islanders towards the end of this period, including slave labour and the use of 'comfort' women by Japanese administrators and servicemen, some positive memories of this relationship remain. Many of the older generation of Marshallese retain Japanese as their second language as opposed to English and Japanese bloodlines persist as a consequence of substantial inter-marriage. This has facilitated recent increased economic interaction with Japan.

In contemporary Marshallese society the main external cultural influences appear to be of American origin. Following the destruction wrought by the Second World War, the USA was charged by the UN with the responsibility of guiding Micronesia towards eventual self-government. The newly formed UN created a Trusteeship Council to administer territories formerly under the control of Japan and the Axis powers.

Micronesia differed from other territories in a similar position as it had the unique designation of being a Strategic Trust Territory. The significance of the Strategic designation was that it gave the USA virtual sovereign control over the Trust Territories of the Pacific Islands (TTPI) because of its power of veto in the UN Security Council.[18] This was especially relevant in relation to the Marshall Islands as a testing site for the US nuclear weapons programme.

During this period the USA received criticism for the lack of support given to the Micronesians to help to rebuild their economies and develop indigenous national administrations. One health concern was an outbreak of polio in the Marshall Islands, but there was a comparatively low prevalence of lifestyle-related diseases at this time.

The Kennedy administration dramatically increased funding for federal programmes in TTPI including US Peace Corps volunteer community workers and scholarships for Marshall Islanders and other Micronesians to undertake higher education in American universities. Many of the elite who benefited from US education later became key government officials.

The US mandate to guide Micronesia towards self-government became secondary to its desire to retain strategic outposts in the Pacific. The transition to an alternative political status for Micronesia involved limited options due to the economic dependency on the USA that had evolved during Trusteeship. It was clear that it was not a viable option to give up all of the US federal grants and additional support offered by this established relationship. It was also clear that the USA wished to maintain a closer relationship with these territories than that of a traditional alliance and to maintain at least the ability to veto any Micronesian policies that would be counter to perceived US interests. To do this the USA pushed for a political status for TTPI that fell short of full independence.

The Marshall Islands, like the Federated States of Micronesia (FSM) and Palau, is currently in a Compact of Free Association with the USA. A 15-year agreement came into force in 1986. This agreement can be seen as a progression from Trusteeship status. The Marshall Islands has international recognition as a sovereign state with UN membership. It is a member of the South Pacific Forum and the Alliance of Small Island States and enters into international negotiations, such as those of the Intergovernmental Panel on Climate Change. Some non-Marshallese are employed in overseas Missions but international relations are generally conducted via the President's office and Foreign Affairs and Trade, which demands new skills of Marshallese officials. The main difference between Free Association and complete political independence is that the USA remains responsible for defence of the Marshall Islands and is obliged to provide substantial amounts of development assistance for the duration of the Compact.

There appears to be little support for complete independence within the Marshall Islands. In part this is due to the historical circumstances that have undermined much of the Marshall Islands' viability as a wholly independent nation. Without substantial overseas investment and assistance it is difficult to see how the Marshall Islands could become self-sufficient. In this respect the Marshall Islands, and the rest of the former TTPI, are almost unique. Predominantly the historical drive of political organization has been to seek political autonomy. New Zealand's Free Association with Niue and the Cook Islands are the only other examples of such a relationship of internal self-government but with defence issues the responsibility of the metropole power. Again the need for economic viability is central to these arrangements. Although there is undoubted national pride in Marshallese identity and heritage, this does not appear to extend to a desire to break away from the dependent relationship with the USA.

By 2001 over US$1 billion will have been provided to the Marshall Islands either via direct grants or federal programmes under the Compact agreement. This constitutes about 75 per cent of the entire Marshallese budget.[19] Without this income the Marshall Islands would have been unable to undertake the vast majority of its current development programmes. These include Air Marshall Islands, the establishment of a tuna export industry and infrastructure including power plants, sewers and a desalination plant. Civil service and health and education budgets would also have been extremely difficult for the Marshall Islands to generate independently. Given the alternative it is hardly surprising that the Marshall Islands' negotiators were willing to accept the US-driven version of the Compact.

The overriding reason why the USA worked so hard to retain this minute territory in a remote part of the Pacific Ocean is that it was of vital strategic importance and had become a central element in its nuclear testing programme. To most of the outside world the Marshall Islands is known almost solely for Bikini Atoll as the former site for US nuclear testing. From 'Operation Crossroads' in 1946 to 'Operation Hardtack' in 1958 a total of 66 tests took place. The issue of relocation of the Bikinians, illness associated with fall-out from the tests, clean-up and resettlement programmes and claims for compensation remain a part of contemporary US–Marshallese relations.[20]

One of the provisions of the Marshall Islands Compact was that the compensation package included was described as a 'full and final settlement' of claims for the negative impact of the test programme. The agreement also states that this point could be looked at again if there were 'changed circumstances'. In light of more recent scientific evidence regarding the detrimental effects of the tests and the Clinton administration's policy of accepting claims from US veterans involved in the test programme, the Marshall Islands is now reviewing its position with regard to these claims. US Energy Secretary Federico Pena has talked of 'righting past wrongs' should studies conclude that the USA was negligent with regard to safety procedures during the testing.[21] This may generate further income but it also reinforces negative stereotypes of a contaminated landscape and of the Marshallese as 'victims' of the bomb.

The international anti-nuclear movement has done much to publicize the plight of the Marshallese suffering displacement and illness associated with the testing. This has had some bearing on the Compact negotiations and there have been suggestions made that Micronesians, particularly in Palau, were using the nuclear issue to gain more favourable terms under the Compact agreement.[22] Regardless of the validity of the claims for compensation they have become one of the key issues as far as international attention on these islands is concerned. In 1995 Lijon Eknilang from Rongelap Atoll in the Marshall Islands testified before the International Court of Justice in the Hague. The Court was considering the legality of the use, or threat of use of nuclear weapons:

> *The most common birth defects on Rongelap and nearby islands have been 'jellyfish' babies. These are born with no bones in their bodies and with transparent skin. We can see their brains and hearts beating. The babies usually live for a day or two, before they stop breathing. Many women die in childbirth or give birth to what look like strands of purple grapes which we quickly hide away and bury.*[23]

Such emotive testimony, plus descriptions of the high incidence of thyroid and other cancers, have played a pivotal role in gaining international support for the Marshallese claims.

In addition to the question of compensation, nuclear issues continue to be relevant to the Marshall Islands. One of the more inventive ideas relating to how the Marshall Islands might generate foreign earnings involves using the former test sites as dumps for nuclear wastes.[24] The logic of this is that as these atolls are already irradiated what better place to locate such waste? As with the whole process of Free Association one of the key features of this proposal is that it must be seen within the context of very limited options for drawing in revenue. Accepting such waste should not be viewed as a preferred choice but as yet another compromise.

Although there is a unique aspect to the Marshall Islands experience as a US nuclear test site and its struggle for compensation, there are comparable situations in other peripheral states. The Uzbek experience, with a legacy of incompetent or malign economic planning leading to the environmental disaster in the Aral Sea region, has some parallels with the position of the Marshallese. It appears to be a characteristic of marginalization that along with inherited disadvantages there are restrictions on what options are available to offset negative situations and to promote positive change.

Marshallese history and more recent political developments go some way towards explaining the limitations of options available to both individuals and community decision makers. Fundamental elements such as geographic isolation and the limited resource base are factors that increase the vulnerability of the Marshallese economy. Since becoming a republic, the Marshall Islands has attempted to assert greater independence and to attract investment and trade with other states, but it has had little success. Increased trade liberalization will only add to the Marshall Islands' economic vulnerability as it attempts to compete in an increasingly aggressive international economic climate.

Broader comparisons with similar patterns of unequal development in various parts of the world can be made. There is clearly an unequal relationship; divisions of wealth are increasing and public options regarding all manner of economic and political decisions are being taken out of the hands of the electorate. As such the US–Marshall Islands relationship can be seen as symbolizing several aspects of contemporary events, at both the individual and community levels. Economies in transition and numerous developing countries throughout the world face similar problems. As economies become increasingly enmeshed, the channelling of resources from periphery to core continues to exacerbate patterns of uneven development. The next chapter focuses on the problems associated with attempting to develop economic and societal wellbeing from a disadvantaged position within a competitive international environment.

Chapter 5

Economic Survival on the Periphery

Chapter 4 showed how peripheral states have become increasingly marginalized by their relationships with more dominant powers. There is an interaction between politics and economics. Many socialist states have radically changed their economic strategies in the last decade. In non-socialist states global economic fluctuations have pushed many into economic crises. These changes have major implications for health and well-being. We now consider adaptations to recent developments in the political and economic climate. This chapter and the next look at recent economic developments and how they have affected population health.

Many developing countries have achieved statehood only to find that they remain heavily dependent on factors relating to the international economic system. Even if they have sovereign control over the manner in which they allocate their national budgetary expenditure, external factors often determine the overall level of funding available. Often this leads to a reduction in welfare expenditure as this is one of the more elastic areas of government responsibility. Some states face restrictions in domestic budgetary controls if they are subject to structural adjustment programmes which set spending criteria to secure loans from the IMF. Generally the criteria for the provision of such loans revolves around increased privatization and reduced government spending, usually in the area of public welfare. Increasing the proportion of economic activity in the private sector reinforces existing economic patterns which restrict political input. That is, the emphasis is purely on profit-making as opposed to meeting community needs, even though privately owned and operated companies may provide social services.

A key element of marginalization is that capitalist development does not meet the societal needs of all citizens. Governments might be unwilling, or unable, to mitigate the more negative effects of such development. Adopting a position whereby market forces supersede social provisions might be viable in the short term, perhaps also in the longer term if marginalized people can be overlooked or their socioeconomic decline can be managed without unduly affecting the broader society. However, longer-term consequences arising from marginalization have detrimental effects, certainly for individuals and eventually for broader society, both domestically and internationally. Apart from any ethical concerns regarding the imposition of undue suffering on greater numbers of people, there is the broader self-interested concern about the overall health of the community and the environment.

Overall economic growth within a state can mask real declines in living standards suffered by individuals and groups marginalized from the potential benefits of development. With growing divisions in wealth, both within and between societies, there is a tendency for economic status to determine social standing and well-being. Despite the increasing significance of economic determinants, cultural factors retain their importance. Most societies have moral fables suggesting that wealth does not necessarily bring happiness. It is clear, however, that wealth does provide a cushion against numerous hardships and does increase the range of options and choices available to individuals.

MONGOLIA

Even after the collapse of the Soviet Empire, the economic legacy from this association remains a determining factor in contemporary Mongolian affairs. Starting in 1948 Mongolia adopted a Five Year Plan cycle. This had far-reaching socioeconomic implications, and accelerated the transition away from the traditional lifestyle of nomadic herding. Urbanization provided a vastly different lifestyle for those used to ranging widely with their herds. It also brought different health concerns. The political economy of the Mongolian people illustrates well how extensively modernization can impact on society and how people are required to adapt to it.

The period of central planning under Soviet tutelage ended with the collapse of the USSR. The Mongolian people then had to contend with the transition to a new and radically different system dominated by market economic forces. Economic reforms to this end hark back to the mid-1980s. Although Soviet forces and technicians did not begin their phased withdrawal until 1989, it was clear that Mongolia, and other satellites of the Soviet system, were preparing for an anticipated transition several years before the subsequent collapse of the Soviet Empire.[1] Undoubtedly the pressure for economic reform in both China and the USSR which existed at that time assisted the process of transition to a market economy in Mongolia. Without such an environment, especially with regard to the USSR, it is likely that the Mongolian government would have had greater difficulty in implementing such sweeping reforms.

The connections between economics and politics are clear in the case of the reforms undertaken in the former Communist bloc states. Years of authoritarian rule, a sense of marginalization from political processes, plus a decline in living standards, led to a popular will for change. Economic necessity, in terms of shortages of basic foodstuffs and medical treatment, led to popular demonstrations for political change and radical economic restructuring. This was matched by a supply of entrepreneurs willing to take advantage of a broad range of market opportunities. In the initial phases of reform the emphasis was on making the command economy more efficient. By 1990 there was an overt policy of shifting to a free-market economy.

Between 1986 and 1989 Mongolia's economic growth averaged around 5 per cent annually.[2] This was higher than might have been expected, as Mongolia's external terms of trade deteriorated during this period. During 1988–1989 there was also a period of unusually dry weather which affected crop production. As a member of the international alliance of command economies, the Council for Mutual Economic Assistance (CMEA), Mongolia was restricted to a fixed contract price for its copper exports. This meant that it was unable to benefit from a rise in world market price for copper at this time. A similar agreement with the USSR meant that it was paying above world market price for the import of petroleum, which accounted for 25 per cent of its total imports. Both of these disadvantageous situations have improved through the 1990s. Mongolia has benefited from the switch to a free-market economy by being able to access cheaper oil imports and to maintain a larger proportion of profits from copper exports than under Soviet influence.

Despite a reasonable national economic performance over the past decade Mongolia has experienced a growing domestic disparity of wealth, health and well-being. Several factors related to economic reform have contributed to this situation. Cutbacks in government expenditure led to fewer employment opportunities in the public sector with unemployment emerging as a social problem as population growth led to new entrants into the labour force. Reduced job opportunities were exacerbated by migration from rural to urban areas. Many agricultural cooperatives faced bankruptcy as their input prices exceeded the market price for their goods. The number of people employed in the agricultural sector dropped from 40 per cent in 1980 to 29 per cent in 1989.[3] The retail prices of selected consumer goods fluctuated to the extent that the producers of certain goods could not maintain their businesses. Although the liberalization of the market allowed certain individuals to rapidly advance their earning potential this was at the expense of reduced standards of living for others.

Societal implications of the transition from a command to a market economy have varied across the Mongolian population. The Mongolian government has attempted to manage this transition with alterations in wage structures and pensions designed to offset the inflationary aspects associated with the prices of many consumer goods. Having removed subsidies from inefficient industries the government redirected some of this money to alleviate problems associated with the relatively rapid transition in economic practices. However, with difficulties arising in maintaining a balanced budget it proved impossible to maintain the standard of social services of the command economy era.

Given the scale of socioeconomic changes that Mongolia has experienced in recent years, the overall state of the economy appears to have survived relatively well. This is in spite of the widespread reorientation of policies and a shift in emphasis that allows far greater free enterprise. Studies by the World Bank and the IMF maintain their focus on overall performance. Other analysts have been more specific in recognizing the problems associated with differential income distributions. Neupert commented that Mongolia has been experiencing a 'deep economic crisis characterised by increasing unemployment, high inflation, shortages of food, and a drastic reduction in government expenditures'.[4] This included expenditure on health and welfare.

Mongolia has some advantages in that it retains large-scale mineral deposits that are competitive on world markets, especially copper. Its vast territory and growing population have immense potential for further development. Moreover, it has retained a strong sense of cultural identity despite years of domination and dependence torn between Chinese and Soviet influences. The transition from a command to a market economy has inevitably had negative consequences for certain groups and individuals. The stress associated with this transition has contributed to a rise in lifestyle-related diseases, as discussed in Chapter 6. This has been exacerbated by the withdrawal of Soviet support, and a virtual collapse of some key elements of welfare provision, notably in the area of health care. These more negative aspects of modernization and economic transition relate the Mongolian experience to other states facing similar circumstances.

UZBEKISTAN

As a member of the former Soviet Union, Uzbekistan has been even more dramatically affected by the collapse than Mongolia because it was more closely tied to the orbit of Soviet influence. The Soviet collapse not only affected the economy but also raised issues of identity and relations with other states, which required a fundamental reorientation for the Uzbek people and government. As with Mongolia, there has been an attempt to minimize the social disruption bought about by the move from a command to a market economy. The creation of the Commonwealth of Independent States has gone some way towards retaining a sense of regional unity, a common ideology and a mutually supportive framework to help manage the impact of modernization and privatization.

The decline in output, disruption of inter-republic trade, loss of subsidies from Moscow and high inflation have all contributed to Uzbekistan's economic difficulties.[5] While Uzbekistan had some advantages over Mongolia in terms of a more developed infrastructure, the level of integration within the Soviet Empire was such that the collapse was no less traumatic, even though the Uzbeks had retained a strong culture throughout more than a century of direct rule from Moscow. Despite the obvious economic difficulties of declining production and markets, the Uzbek government was, like Mongolia, able to draw on nationalist sentiments and rhetoric to mobilize popular support. To some extent this support went through a 'honeymoon period', which was reflected in other former Soviet Republics. Despite the rejection of communism for failing to provide for the needs of the general population, and in some instances for being corrupt, support for the newly independent regimes was mixed. Understandably support tended to be divided between which groups and individuals benefited or were disadvantaged by changed circumstances.

As in many developing countries, Uzbek society has retained its communal identity, even during the Soviet period. The new government has made use of this in a recent development in which local neighbourhood associations, known as 'mahallas' now organize publicly funded community activities, such as repairs to homes and roads, in which all adult residents take part. The mahallas are also used to identify the needy and distribute welfare assistance. The government is increasingly relying on these groups to promote aspects of social development as well.[6] This reflects a global trend as increased economic liberalization is mirrored by the 'retreat of the state' in providing social care.

In January 1994 Uzbekistan's President Karimov issued a decree entitled 'On Measures for Further Deepening Economic Reforms, Providing for the Protection of Private Property and for the Development of Entrepreneurship'.[7] Here he outlined five basic principles for economic reforms: priority of economy over politics; leadership of the State as the main reform-maker; a solid legal framework; social protection; and step by step transition to a market economy. The first of these principles demonstrates an unequivocal policy orientation towards development driven by proposed economic growth. This was to be the 'touchstone' from which all other policies would flow.

Before 1994 many consumer goods such as food, housing, transport, energy and health care were heavily subsidised by Moscow. The World Bank estimated that such subsidies accounted for 21 per cent of GDP in 1993.[8] Although Uzbekistan had one of the best resource bases within the former USSR, it still experienced difficulties in maintaining these subsidies. Between December 1991 and January 1992 retail prices rose by 120 per cent.[9] As with the Mongolian experience, the cost to consumers was offset to some extent by the restructuring of wages, pensions and other state benefits. However, this was insufficient to avoid a decline in real living standards for some of the population.

As with most economies in transition, Uzbekistan turned to Western economic institutions to provide economic advice and assistance. Structural adjustment programmes were introduced with the aim of better managing the growth of liberalization and privatization.[10] As in other states where such programmes have been introduced, the emphasis has been on developing the private sector, often at the cost of welfare provision. Not all sectors of the society can simultaneously benefit from such measures. Even allowing for some wider dispersal of income generated under such a scheme there will be, at best, a delay before such benefits spread throughout society. More likely, as evidence from most states suggests, benefits will accrue to the higher and middle income brackets, with the poorest sectors of society becoming increasingly marginalized.[11]

Both Mongolia and Uzbekistan have great potential wealth in their natural and human resources. Their experiences under Soviet influence have clearly been mixed, but neither were adequately prepared for a smooth transition to a liberal market economy. The socioeconomic convulsions that have accompanied this change have had diverse impacts throughout both societies.

THE MARSHALL ISLANDS

The Marshall Islands' experience further illustrates the difficulties faced by peripheral states. Unlike Mongolia and Uzbekistan, the Marshall Islands have not been compelled to make a sudden transition to a different type of economy, and it is unlikely that there will be any radical change in economic philosophy in the future. However, the potential reduction of Compact funding in 2001 is likely to have a profound effect. Lifestyle options in the Marshall Islands are influenced by a broad range of factors, the most important being economic issues and political control. Government spending priorities are generally determined by available finances.

Despite the continuance of the traditional clan and class system, the overlay of a cash economy has had a profound impact on most aspects of Marshallese life. For those that were already wealthy and subsequently retained their position, the transition was relatively smooth. They could afford to meet their material needs in the past and continue to do so. Problems arise for those who had previously relied on a communally supported subsistence system. Subsistence has declined due to a combination of rising expectations and rapid population growth. The shift to a cash economy has required a radical adjustment in lifestyles. This includes place of residence, adjusting to reliance on a cash income, coping when there is no wage-earner, managing household tasks around working hours, adjusting child care and generally fitting in with a society that has undertaken a widespread change in the way in which it is organized. This reorganization also includes some alteration in norms and values, especially in relation to position in the workforce and social standing. Such changes are less dramatic in the remoter atolls, but they have a marked impact on most Marshallese.

The relationship between politics and economics is a universal dilemma for policy-makers. In Pacific island cultures there is an expectation that traditional leaders, or their contemporary equivalents, who are often one and the same, will provide for the wider community. With a growing population and an economy in recession it is increasingly difficult for the contemporary Marshallese leaders to fulfil these expectations. Also, to some extent, economic dependence on the USA has undermined chiefly power. For the most part the traditional rights and duties of the Paramount Chief and Council of Chiefs remain intact, but the USA now provides virtually all welfare and most material goods.

Throughout the period of Trusteeship the Marshall Islands became increasingly dependent on US Federal programmes and the wages arising from an expansive public sector. There was little incentive for either the public or private sectors to break free from this situation. Except for the campaign for nuclear test compensation, the main political activities in the region were inward looking and focused on domestic rivalries. Although an outsider might perceive Marshallese culture as non-confrontational, there are numerous internal conflicts and competitions. Disputes relating to land tenure and the rights that arise from land ownership are common. Similarly the opportunities for personal aggrandizement and gain that have arisen for the managers of Compact funds have also led to some resentment, both from other politicians and the general public.

The Compact allows independent control of national financial affairs, and the Marshall Islands has internal self-government, but this does not necessarily mean economic autonomy. This is because of continuing dependence on US economic assistance. This dependence is increasing as population growth continues to outstrip economic growth and job creation. The influx of Compact funding since the mid-1980s has failed to off-set the constraints of a narrow resource base, poor infrastructure development, distance from markets and the need to repay international loans which used the pending Compact funding as collateral. This has led to declining economic performances.

World Bank figures indicate a decline in average annual growth (real GDP) from 8.7 per cent between 1980/81 and 1986/87 to 0.3 per cent between 1986/87 and 1991/92.[12] This sharp change in growth rate occurred precisely when the Marshall Islands economy received the first tranche of Compact funding. Although the global trend was for some decline in the late 1980s, the decline was more dramatic in the Marshall Islands because of its inability to fall back on reserves or to diversify into other potential areas of growth.

One of the key principles behind the Compact agreement has been that the 15 years it is due to run should be a transition period from Trusteeship to full economic viability and independence. This idea is reflected in the 'step down' principle whereby funding is reduced by US$5 million every five years. The expectation was that the Marshall Islands should be able to match this reduction by either attracting alternative foreign investment or generating its own income earning projects. To date this target has yet to be achieved.

A major disappointment for the Marshall Islands has been its inability to attract significant overseas investment. This has not been for the want of trying. In 1989 a guide for potential investors was produced.[13] Suggested investment opportunities included commercial livestock operations, production of fruit and vegetables, fish cannery, aquaculture, tourist resorts, manufacturing and light assembly work, construction, telecommunication and airline services and the possibility of the privatization of government services. Tax incentives were offered; most of the above businesses paying no income tax for the first five years of operations. Some investment has been forthcoming but in insufficient quantities to replace Compact funding.

The Marshall Islands has tremendously valuable marine resources, but is unable to exploit them domestically. Sale of fishing licences has generated income, predominantly from Japan, but the bulk of the profit from this resource is exported with the fish. Capital has not been sought to establish a locally owned ocean-going fishing fleet. Rather the government has allowed Japan, China and Taiwan to exploit local fishing resources in return for lease payments which are equivalent to only a small payout of the potential profit. Similarly the potential wealth of sea-bed resources can only be exploited via licensing agreements. To date technological constraints have prevented such exploitation but it is hoped that exploratory operations may begin in the early part of the 21st century. With limited response from overseas investors the Marshall Islands has been unable to balance its budget because it has to rely on its own underdeveloped economic activities. Again this situation can be found in many developing states.

Like many developing nations, in the Marshall Islands the main growth in employment has been in the public sector. Although there are some successful local entrepreneurs, the overall balance of public and private sector employment is weighted towards government or government-related jobs. In 1995 just over 4000 were employed in the public sector and 4700 in the private sector.[14] That is, nearly half of the labour force was in what are effectively administrative positions. In 1986 only 2600 were in the public sector and 4400 in the private sector.

Compact funds pay the salaries of most public sector employees. A similar pattern can be found in other dependent countries, such as Papua New Guinea, which relies on Australian economic assistance to meet most of its public service salaries. In 1997 the Marshallese government cut 150 government jobs in an effort to reduce this dependence on Compact funding, and more cuts are expected. This is a significant reduction in urban employment, and has brought hardship to families reliant on an income from this source. It also has repercussions in other sectors by reducing the effective demand for goods.

There has been no serious attempt and little opportunity to pursue a policy of import substitution. Each arrival of a container ship adds to the availability of imported goods in local supermarkets, many of which are prohibitively expensive for most of the population. The marked lack of a manufacturing sector, with the exception of the production of handicrafts, similarly contributes to the impression that a balance of payments deficit will continue for the foreseeable future. Although exports rose sharply in 1994/95, due almost entirely to a chilled and frozen fish operation, this still left a deficit of nearly US$52 million.[15] Despite record exports of US$23 million in 1995, imports also rose to a new high of US$75 million in the same year. In part the rise in imports could be explained by population growth. Throughout the 1990s over one-quarter of all imports were food, and up until 1994 this was the largest percentage of imports by value. In 1995 mineral fuels and lubricants became the highest percentage of imports by value, at US$22.5 million or 30 per cent. Again this can be linked to a growing population and an increased demand for energy.

The Marshall Islands' remoteness adds to shipping and handling costs. It also reduces the range of goods suitable for importation. Improvements in freezing and chilling technologies have meant that more fresh produce can be imported. But, again, there are cost implications. The hot climate makes it difficult to handle perishable foods. The need to keep food fresh adds to energy demand. The majority of food imports are either frozen, canned or dried. Some are also packaged as convenience 'ready meals'. As discussed elsewhere in this book many have poor nutritional value and are closely related to the degenerative diseases associated with poor diet. Not only are many of the imported foodstuffs unhealthy but they are also uneconomic and a major contributor to the growing balance of payments deficit. An obvious way to reduce this deficit, and to improve the nation's health, would be to replace imports with more locally produced food, but this would require a change in preferences and a willingness to give up imported consumer goods.

The importation of oil is another drain on the economy. The bulk of the Marshall Islands' energy demands are met via two oil-burning power stations, on Majuro and Ebeye. This is a very inefficient method of electricity production. Cheaper renewable alternatives exist in the form of solar and wind power generation. Wave power is at present expensive, but represents a possible future energy source. Under-investment in these technologies means that, at present, unit costs for renewable energy systems are still high but will reduce as the scale of development improves.

The Marshall Islands has already experimented with solar-powered units on remote atolls with some success. Similarly, wind-power generators would be suitable low-cost sources of energy in isolated areas. Although there remains ongoing debate regarding the cost-effectiveness of various alternative energy supplies, they are the subject of worldwide research, and designs are improving. There is considerable opportunity to expand this aspect of energy provision in the Marshall Islands, but capital investment in appropriate technology is required. The demand for energy, as for food, grows with population. Unlike many developed states there are fewer opportunities to reduce energy use. Heating and lighting are minor components in the energy budget and it is difficult to reduce air conditioning in the interests of comfort and productivity. However, air conditioning would be less of a drain on expenditure if it were powered by renewable energy.

As with the difficulty in adopting an import substitution policy, the Marshall Islands does not have the capital investment potential to start large export industries. Fish processing and packaging could potentially be a successful export operation. Instead the government has allowed Chinese entrepreneurs to develop this industry. In 1994/95 chilled fish production was valued at US$12.6 million of which Marshall Islands derived US$8.4 million. This is a reasonable return, but less than could have been achieved had the operation been entirely Marshallese, and there were fewer multiplier effects since the Chinese employed their own labour.

Previous attempts at large-scale national businesses have not proved very successful. The national airline, Air Marshall Islands, has not been as profitable as hoped and its operations have been scaled down. In part this has been due to competition from a US airline, Continental, but also reflects the difficulty a small island state has in managing large-scale projects. Nauru experienced similar problems with its own airline. In a small fleet there is no backup for aircraft grounded by mechanical problems. Also there is a limited pool of potential staff for both flight crew and ground support technicians. If overseas expertise is called on to fill such positions the running costs are prohibitively high. Local training is possible but, again, would require very substantial investment. The poor performance of the airline plus the lack of return from other investments has increased the need to develop the export sector, although to date this has only had minimal success.

The Marshall Islands' exports consist almost solely of copra (coconut-based) products. Apart from copra there is also a small export market for handicraft goods and another for pet fish. More recently, clam farming for the overseas aquarium market and artificial pearl cultivation have been developed.[16] Again this relates to the problems of transport costs for both production inputs and distance from markets. Marshallese attitudes towards resources and planning are indicated in a comment made by the owner of the clam farming operation. He said that the reason they concentrated on the aquarium market was that farming for clam meat was uneconomic because it takes about 50 years to reach maturity. Interestingly, locally supplied wild clam meat is always available in the store owned by the same businessman. Although in some areas of the Marshall Islands wild clams are taken from the reef at levels which are sustainable relative to the time they take to mature, respondents reported that this was not the norm and clam resources were being depleted. There were similar concerns raised about the depletion of fisheries due to overfishing, the taking of immature fish which reduced the reproductive capacity of the stock, and pollution from the dumping of rubbish and sewage outflow.

Copra production is clearly insufficient as a basis for economic expansion. Moreover, if the value of the crop is artificially maintained via subsidies the real value of copra exports is reduced. It is also doubtful whether current levels of production can be maintained. Some of the trees are producing smaller and fewer coconuts than in the past because they are reaching the end of their productive lives. Previous agricultural development programmes have shown that production can be increased but it requires forward planning and a programme of replanting.[17] Similar planning could also increase the production of fruit and vegetable crops. Although it is unlikely that these would form additional exports they could find a domestic market, and at the same time give the urban population better access to fresh food.

One domestic enterprise is a water purification plant on Majuro. Initially a relatively small operation, the purification plant has expanded to meet consumer demand. The same company has taken the lead in developing ecotourism to the outer islands. In conjunction with this it runs a scuba diving operation that also emphasizes the need to protect the marine habitat. Such operations are encouraging, but few in number, and few Marshallese benefit from them. Although this business is contributing to national revenue via taxation, it does not employ many Marshallese because its activities are not generally labour intensive. Moreover, it tends to employ foreign workers when special skills are required, such as scuba diving masters. As with the example of airline pilots, these positions could be filled by appropriately skilled Marshallese if they were available.

Another potential source of employment for Marshallese was a garment factory proposed by Chinese investors. When these plans were originally discussed there were hopes in the Marshall Islands that a local labour force would be recruited. Now it seems that if this project goes ahead the majority of workers will be Chinese. A similar situation arose in Yap in the late 1980s when another garment factory operated using a foreign labour force. Investors are willing to bring in their own workers, either because they can undercut local pay scales or they lack faith in the abilities of the local workforce.

In the absence of manufactured goods or substantial primary products, the Marshall Islands has sought other means of generating foreign earnings. As with other small island states, the sale of postage stamps has been profitable. Peaking at US$408,841 in 1990 these sales continue to hover around US$150,000 per annum. More controversial has been the sale of passports, especially to Chinese nationals. This trade has faltered since the USA made it clear that such passports would not automatically grant entry to America. Another more successful venture has been as a port of registration for foreign ships. This flag of convenience operation is run as a joint venture with the US-based International Registries Inc. Half the ships registered are owned by US companies, and the second largest group is Greek. Mobil Oil has two supertankers flying the Marshall Islands flag. For 1997 the revenue from this source was US$331,000, and there are indications that this operation will continue to expand. There is growing international concern regarding the stringency of safety standards onboard oil tankers. The flag of convenience policy of some states does appear to have involved a decline in standards. At present the Marshall Islands would have difficulty in independently inspecting and certifying the safety of these tankers, as it would need to train inspectors. As this is a joint venture with a US company, presumably these safety procedures are managed by appropriately trained staff. Where this not the case, the Marshall Islands could risk substantial losses if it were found to be negligent following an oil spill or similar event.

The local retail structure and the type and availability of goods for sale, affects local food production, diet and the general transition to a cash economy. Despite the poor balance of payments situation within the Marshall Islands, TTPI and Compact funding have ensured that there has been a circulation of money within the economy. A combination of public and private employment has meant that, even with limited jobs per household, there have been sufficient wages available to generate a vigorous retailing sector.

This has been based on the substitution of food previously grown locally and satisfying the desire to join in the consumption of Western produced material goods. These range from electrical appliances through to disposable nappies. Even so, many of these goods are unaffordable for most Marshallese who are either unemployed or poorly paid. The strong social ethic of sharing with relatives means that even those who are employed do not always enjoy high personal levels of disposable income.

Retail outlets in the Marshall Islands are essentially controlled by five wholesale companies. These have their own stores and supply the vast majority of other outlets in Majuro, Ebeye and the outer islands. Most outer islands have a greater reliance on locally produced foodstuffs because they are readily available and because the supply of goods from Majuro is irregular. In general a core–periphery model operates, with the more remote atolls relying more on traditional subsistence lifestyles, although lifestyles and eating habits change rapidly when the establishment of an airstrip allows for a greater variety and bulk of consumer goods to be shipped in. As this trend continues, subsistence practices are being undermined, although generally Marshallese residing in the outer islands still have the capability to return to subsistence if necessary. On Ebeye and Majuro, however, lack of space and complex patterns of land ownership and also the difficulty of leasing land restrict opportunities to return to subsistence cultivation.

It is commonly believed in the Marshall Islands that US acceptance of greater responsibility for the ill-effects of the nuclear test programme would translate into an extension of the Compact. In view of the poor economic performance of the Marshall Islands since 1986, there is no great expectation from the USA that further funding will be put to any better use. Compensation for nuclear testing and the rental agreement for the Kwajalein missile range could be dealt with independently of other economic concerns. If the USA were to decide to terminate the Compact and the associated economic assistance it would have disastrous implications for the Marshallese economy.

The case of the Marshall Islands has many parallels with other developing countries on the periphery of the global economy which aspire to a Western consumer lifestyle. Many have experienced rapid population growth, distorted development and resource depletion. When a global recession and falling commodity prices rob them of their main sources of revenue they can find themselves unable to pay the wages of their public sector employees, unable to import the goods they demand and unable to ensure that basic needs are met. Yet they may have been prevented from developing a secure economic basis by their marginalized position in relation to the core states.

Even though many developing countries believe that their lives have been improved by the limited modernization they have experienced, in reality they have often made few gains in terms of health and well-being. This is because factors such as limited investment in social services, poverty and inequality prevent the achievement of an optimal lifestyle. In addition a misunderstanding of the consequences of the type of lifestyle they have adopted may mean the development of new and serious health problems. The following chapters focus on health issues and the way in which they have been affected by the process of modernization. In particular, they consider the negative impacts on health experienced by those who are denied the potential benefits of modernization because of their location on the periphery.

Chapter 6

Population and Health in Socialist Peripheral Countries

The three countries that are the focus of this study have all experienced changes in their health patterns as a consequence of their contact with more developed nations. However, so far none of them has completed a transition to a pattern in which infectious diseases are largely controlled, life expectancy is long and the main causes of death are NCDs occurring at older ages. This chapter and the following chapter examine the nature of the changes which have occurred, and the factors which have prevented a complete health transition in each of the three countries. Each case study begins with a brief sketch of the population characteristics, and then examines the influence of peripheral locations on the external and sociological determinants of population health.

MONGOLIA

Population

In 1994 Mongolia's population was estimated as 2.25 million, assuming an annual average growth rate of 1.8 per cent since the 1989 census count of 2,043,954. In 1918 the population total was only 647,500. It increased only slowly until the 1950s, when a dramatic reduction in mortality, coupled with continuing high fertility, produced annual growth rates of more than 2 per cent, climbing to almost 3 per cent in the 1970s.[1] Some 81 per cent of the people belong to the Hahl ethnic group, 6 per cent are Hasags, and almost 3 per cent are Durveds, with small numbers belonging to a further 20 or so ethnic groups, mostly living in rural areas. By 1989 only 247 Chinese and 140 Russians were resident in Mongolia, although numbers would have been much higher in periods of closer association with these countries. Some 55 per cent of the population live in urban areas, while the remainder are semi-nomadic rural herdsmen. The capital city, Ulaanbaatar, had 525,000 inhabitants in 1989, and was more than six times as large as Darhan, the second largest city. The mining town of Erdenet ranked third with 46,000 people.[2]

Early censuses indicated total fertility rates (TFRs) of six or seven children per woman, and as recently as 1980 the TFR was still 6.4. By 1985 this had declined to 5.5, then to 4.3 in 1990 and 2.5 in 1993. This is a very rapid decline by any standard, and reflects the serious deterioration in Mongolia's economic conditions as the Soviet Empire crumbled. Life expectancy at birth was estimated as 64 years in 1995, having increased from only 48 in 1960, but this is largely attributable to a falling birth rate and a relative increase in those least at risk, since there has been little progress in reducing infant mortality.[3]

Mongolia uses the Soviet definition of a live birth, which excludes those dying in the first seven days after delivery. Official estimates of the infant mortality rate (IMR) can therefore be considered as understatements. Even so, the IMR is reported to have increased from 79 deaths per thousand live births in 1969 to 89 in 1984. It appears to have declined since the 1980s, with official figures stating an IMR of 61 for 1993, but other sources using the conventional definition of a live birth estimated 76 per thousand.[4] The latest official Mongolian estimates available at the time of writing suggest a further decline to only 41 by 1996, but some observers suggest that this is unlikely in view of deteriorating health conditions, and could underestimate actual infant deaths by as much as 50 per cent.[5]

A source of concern is an increase in maternal mortality rates in the 1990s, despite falling fertility. Again the estimates vary markedly between sources. UNICEF estimates an average of 240 deaths per 100,000 live births for the period 1980–92, while the official estimates are 140 for the period 1985–89 and 177 for 1996.[6] Regardless of the actual numbers used, it is known that there has been a deterioration in maternal services and an increase in unsafe abortions.

The combination of sharply declining fertility and high infant mortality has produced a reasonably well balanced age structure, with 39 per cent aged less than 15 years, 57 per cent of working age and 4 per cent aged 65 or more. Projections of future population growth on the basis of sustained low fertility predict a population of 3.4 million by 2019, or 4.1 million if fertility returns to 1990 levels.[7]

At the foundation of the Mongolian People's Republic the government adopted a policy of population expansion as part of the drive to modernize the country and to develop natural resources. Soviet-style pro-natalist strategies were adopted, such as promoting large family sizes, honouring women for bearing large families and ensuring that contraception was not widely available. By 1989 an increasing understanding of population and gender issues led to the removal of restrictions on the importation of contraceptives, and the United Nations Population Fund launched a five-year programme to support a family planning programme based in the Ministry of Health.[8]

Even so, there is still a pro-natalist interest group in Mongolia, which includes some politicians. This group argues that Mongolia needs greater population numbers to deter China from expanding into thinly populated Mongolian lands, a view which has received increasing support in recent years as a consequence of the dramatic fertility decline. The existence of conflicting views about population growth have weakened Mongolia's commitment to family planning, and the family planning programme has not been widely promoted. Another deterrent is that women with less than three children have to pay for contraceptives, which leads many to opt for the one-time expense of an IUD, a method associated with a high incidence of side effects. At the same time there are often shortages of hormonal methods and condoms, especially in rural areas.[9]

Health

Mongolia's present day health system has developed since independence brought a closer association with the USSR. Prior to 1924, Buddhist lamas were virtually the only providers of health care in Mongolia, offering treatments based on Indian, Tibetan and Chinese traditional medicine, as well as local Mongolian cures.

With the establishment of the Mongolian Peoples' Republic a modern Western medical system was adopted, based on the Russian health care model. The Mongolian health system thus reflects the typical socialist pattern, with a strong emphasis on curative rather than preventive medicine.

Mongolian health care is based on a clearly defined hierarchy of medical facilities. In 1992 there were 12 major hospitals (five in Ulaanbaatar), 311 district hospitals, 54 physician posts (clinics) and 1142 feldshers posts (aid posts). In addition, there were various other small facilities capable of delivering limited health services, including physician outposts, various X-ray and other diagnosis posts, and 215 crèches with beds. Public health is monitored by sanitary and epidemiological stations, of which there were 50 in 1992.[10] Health services were essentially free until 1992, although patients were required to pay for medicines from 1990 onwards. Medical insurance was introduced in 1993.[11]

Although the structure of the health system is sound and there is a good network of health facilities, it has some deficiencies. Many of the facilities are staffed only by nurses or paramedics, and there is a shortage of fully trained doctors, especially in rural areas, where the quality and availability of services is generally inferior to urban areas. For example, although the national average was almost three doctors per thousand population, the urban mean is five,[12] while one doctor was reported to be serving a population of 2775 in Hovd administrative district in the remote western Uvs province.[13] Rural populations were comparatively less disadvantaged in terms of access to hospital beds, with 10 per thousand population compared with 13 in urban areas in 1992.

Morbidity rates have been increasing in recent years, reversing the trend prior to 1993. The pattern of disease is characterized by a mix of infectious, parasitic and NCDs. Common infectious and parasitic diseases include viral hepatitis, tuberculosis, scabies and other skin diseases, genito-urinary diseases, respiratory diseases and, since 1994, meningococcal infections. The incidence of sexually transmitted diseases is also said to be increasing rapidly.[14] The predominant NCDs are cardiovascular, digestive and disorders of the nervous system and sensory organs. Hepatitis contributes to high rates of liver disease and cancer. The prevalence of mental illnesses, including schizophrenia, is also high, occurring more than twice as frequently as neoplasms in 1992.[15] This was at least a 250 per cent increase compared with the years up to 1990.

Mongolia is thus characterized by a pattern of uneven progress in health, and general population health cannot be considered to be good. This is primarily due to external factors and, to a lesser extent, to sociological factors which have been exacerbated by external factors. First, Mongolia's health care system is no longer appropriate to the country's needs because it emphasizes curative rather than preventive medicine. Second, Mongolia's peripheral location in the Soviet sphere of influence led to the development of a socioeconomic environment which is not conducive to good population health, while the transition to a market economy has eroded health advances made in the past. Third, traditional Mongolian lifestyles and diets are not conducive to good health, while the transition to a market economy has contributed to a decline in food production. We now look in detail at how these factors have contributed to uneven progress in health.

An inappropriate health care model

The health care system adopted by Mongolia is based on the Soviet model, which is widely recognized as emphasizing curative medicine and neglecting preventive medicine. Although this may have been a universal characteristic of health systems in the past, preventive medicine has become increasingly important in the post-war period. It has been enshrined as a core strategy in world health since the Alma Ata Declaration of 1978 endorsed primary health care. It seems, however, that the primary health care model, which promotes a community-based, 'grass roots' approach to improve health, is incompatible with the centralized control of the health system favoured by Mongolia and some other socialist states.

Neupert points out that a major weakness of Mongolia's approach to health was the lack of community participation in health care. All budgetary, design and management aspects of health care facilities were controlled by central government, without involving local communities.[16] The alienation of health care from the people was exacerbated by the suppression of religion as part of a broader political process. In 1937 lamas were forbidden to practise traditional medicine, and persecuted or driven out of the country. Although some remained and continued providing services secretly, for the most part the people lost the traditional health care provided by the lamas.[17] As a consequence, a totally new health system was imposed, rather than grafting new approaches on to an existing system, which would have facilitated acceptance and understanding of modern medicine.

Aside from compulsory immunization and quarantine measures, the main preventive medical strategy adopted in Mongolia was mandatory examinations of the population by mobile medical teams. This became a type of medical policing system, which imposed health care on the population. It thus inhibited the development of awareness that health is an individual and community responsibility, and communities can work together to improve living conditions. As a consequence, primary health care initiatives such as hygiene and nutrition education, improvement of local sanitation and environments are lacking.[18] Even so, in 1997 UNDP prioritized the most pressing health needs as promoting sterile injection practices, improving the cold chain system to support the immunization programme by ensuring that vaccines are delivered to clinics in good condition, and improving disease surveillance.[19]

Another weakness has been limited and poor-quality maternal and child health care, which is a major factor contributing to the continuing high infant mortality rate and high maternal mortality. As mentioned earlier in this chapter, until 1989 contraception was generally unavailable or limited to intrauterine devices (IUDs). Abortion was used as the main method of averting births, although it was technically illegal until 1989.[20] In 1995 an educated woman in her 30s in Ulaanbaatar told one of the authors that before joining the staff of an international health agency, she had never discussed contraception with anyone and knew nothing about it at all.

Unwanted pregnancies and abortion contribute to depletion, anaemia and generally poor health among women of child bearing age. Even at the time of writing, many rural Mongolians have poor access to contraception and prevalence rates are said to be low. The recent decline in fertility appears to have been due to abstinence and abortion more than to contraception, so women's health may not have benefited greatly from lower fertility. Also it is claimed that the legalization of abortion has made abortion procedures increasingly hazardous, because it has led to an increase in the number of doctors performing abortions in unsanitary conditions and late in pregnancy.[21]

The impact of marginalization and the transition to a market economy

Mongolia's recent transition to a market economy has been marked by a reduction of public expenditure on social services. Absolute expenditure on health declined from US$1.2 million in 1985 to US$1.05 million in 1990 and US$0.37 million in 1992.[22] Between 1991 and 1997 expenditure on health was cut by 42 per cent.[23] This has led to a significant deterioration of the quality and availability of services, especially in rural areas. Aspects of this included closure of facilities, increased use of unskilled staff, shortages of medicines and equipment and declining standards of hygiene.

As well as the specific effect on health expenditure, worsening economic conditions affected health by preventing the development and maintenance of infrastructure such as transport links. In 1994 a UNDP evaluation team concluded 'the deterioration in access to transport is one of the most serious threats to the health care system in rural areas'.[24] Even where a health care facility exists, people may be prevented from using it if they cannot reach it without great difficulty and, when it is far away, if they cannot find somewhere affordable to stay on arrival.

The provision of adequate housing, sanitation, safe water and waste disposal has also lagged far behind population needs. Urban areas are affected by industrial pollution and the inadequate disposal of hazardous wastes. Thirty-eight per cent of the water supplied to urban areas is estimated to be of sub-standard quality because of both chemical and bacterial pollution. Inadequate and malfunctioning water treatment plants discharge untreated sewage into the Tuul River, which flows through Ulaanbaatar, and is estimated to have 2–3.5 times the acceptable levels of nitrogen, phosphate and organic pollution.[25]

Although urban dwellers employed in the state sector are provided with residential apartments, and those employed in private enterprise can afford to pay rent for accommodation, many others who are less privileged live in settlements of 'gerhs' clustered on the edges of cities and towns. Gerhs remain the main form of housing in rural areas. Sanitation is perhaps less important where herdsmen are mobile and frequently relocate gehrs, and where water can be drawn from unpolluted streams and lakes in low population density areas. In contrast, semi-permanent gerh settlements quickly become a health hazard unless they are provided with proper services. There are extensive gerh settlements on the edge of Ulaanbaatar, for example, which are not served by sewage and water systems. Even the water supplied to permanent buildings in Ulaanbaatar is not potable.

A significant factor in child growth is diarrhoeal disease caused by unsafe water and sanitation. A 1992 survey of child health and nutrition found that 28 per cent of children living in gerhs were stunted (significantly below the expected height range for their age), compared with 23 per cent of children living in apartments. This implies not only nutritional disadvantage but also a greater prevalence of diarrhoeal disease.[26]

One positive feature in present day Mongolian health is a revival of interest in traditional medicine and the relaxation of restrictions on traditional healers. New traditional healers are being trained, and since 1990 traditional medicine has been available as a specialization in the Mongolian Medical School.[27] Aside from the possible benefits of traditional medicine per se, there are very positive benefits in that the more caring approach of traditional healers may help to restore confidence in health care. A network of traditional healers could also provide a basis for improved services which incorporate both traditional and modern medicine, with traditional healers providing the first point of contact and referring cases where necessary.

Traditional Mongolian lifestyles and diets

Several aspects of traditional Mongolian lifestyles are not conducive to good health. One is the typical diet, which is high in meat, animal fats and flour, and generally deficient in fruit and vegetables. Crop production is limited by the harsh climate, and over winter only root crops, bread and preserved vegetables are available to supplement animal products. Even in present day Ulaanbaatar, where many people can afford to buy imported food, fresh fruit and vegetables are often in short supply and food tends to be monotonous. As a consequence of the neglect of nutritional education and primary health care there is a general lack of knowledge about the importance of a balanced diet.[28] The typical Mongolian diet contributes to an increased risk of cardiovascular disease. Preservatives used in vegetables and meats can also contribute to carcinomas and digestive diseases.

The transition to a market economy has increased poverty and contributed to loss of food security. Worsening economic conditions have increased the incidence of absolute caloric deficiency with many people consuming fewer calories than they need to survive in the severe Mongolian climate. Food production per capita has declined markedly. Compared with 1990, per capita production of meat in 1996 was 8 per cent less, eggs 88 per cent less, cereals 73 per cent less, potatoes 69 per cent less and vegetables 49 per cent less. Of the major food items only milk production had increased, by a meagre 3 per cent.[29] These reductions have been caused by the near collapse of the cropping sector, degradation of grazing land and increased winter exposure of livestock coupled with decreased availability of winter feed resulting in a reduction in herd numbers. This has caused food security at the national level to become more dependent on world market price movements and the importation of basic food items. In fact Mongolia's terms of trade have become less favourable, and international cereal prices have increased in recent years.[30]

Nutrition surveys in the 1990s indicate that pregnant women may consume 25 per cent less than the recommended intake for Mongolian conditions.[31] Child nutrition is also poor, with deficiencies of vitamin D, iodine and iron, and protein malnutrition being especially common. Rickets is a widespread problem as a consequence of vitamin D deficiency, largely due to the practice of swaddling small children in winter so that they receive no exposure to sunlight. Like many other inland locations, Mongolian soils are generally deficient in iodine, but iodized products such as salt have not been made generally available, either as part of the health system or the retailing pattern. Iodine deficiency manifests as endemic goitre, which affected over 60 per cent of children aged eight or more surveyed in 1989.[32] Iron deficiency is widespread among both children and mothers. Other concerns are late initiation of breast-feeding and early weaning.[33]

Mongolians have traditionally consumed alcoholic beverages, including fermented mare's milk (koomiz), which contributes to an elevated risk of alcoholism and also to digestive tract infections associated with unhygienic preparation. Both men and women appear to be equally at risk of being affected by these conditions. Contemporary urban Mongolians more commonly consume beer and spirits, and heavy drinking and tobacco smoking are common and serious health concerns. The deterioration of economic conditions since the transition to a market economy has been associated with an increasing incidence of alcoholism among men, contributing to family breakdown and exacerbating poverty among women and children. This has led to an increase in the number of female headed households, which tend to be seriously disadvantaged.[34]

Another feature of traditional Mongolian lifestyles which contributes to poor health is the gerh. The impact of the gerh on health is not only the high probability that it lacks safe water and sanitation as discussed in the previous section; it is also likely to be associated with crowding, poor ventilation and a high probability of disease transmission among occupants. Harsh climatic conditions can confine Mongolians to their gerhs for days at a time. Prolonged exposure to smoky environments caused by the wood stove heater and cooker, promotes respiratory disease. Genito-urinary tract diseases, including gall stones, are also associated with gerh living conditions when toilet facilities are absent.

Other aspects of traditional Mongolian lifestyles also affect health. For example, herders who must sit on horseback for many hours in cold climatic conditions are frequently affected by rheumatism. Although many urban Mongolians are no longer affected by such problems, they remain significant among the 45 per cent of Mongolians still in rural areas.

It is thus evident that Mongolia's marginal position vis-à-vis the Soviet core and the difficulties of transition to a market economy have resulted in uneven progress in health. In the 1990s marginalization has had an increasingly negative impact on the external determinants of health, and has exacerbated the less healthy aspects of traditional Mongolian culture and society. This has eroded much of the progress in health made before the transition. As a consequence Mongolia has failed to complete its health transition, and the majority of the population have experienced little improvement in health and well-being.

We now consider the case of Uzbekistan. This country was generally in an advantageous position compared with Mongolia, in that it has a more hospitable geographic location with a better agricultural endowment and a longer history of settlement and cultivation. In addition, it was in a more favourable political situation than Mongolia, as it was a full member of the USSR and thus an integral part of the Soviet economic system and a recipient of substantial Soviet investment in economic and social development.

UZBEKISTAN

Population

In terms of population numbers, Uzbekistan is almost ten times the size of Mongolia. The total population was 22,192,000 in January 1995, and estimated as 22.6 million in 1997. As a consequence of its richer agricultural endowment, Uzbekistan is less urbanized than Mongolia, with approximately 60 per cent living in rural areas. The capital, Tashkent, had a population of 2,113,000 in 1995, which is almost equal to the entire Mongolian population. Other major cities are Samarkand, Bukhara, Andizhan and Ferghana. About three-quarters of Uzbekistan's population belong to the Uzbek ethnic group, 6.5 per cent are Russian and the rest are from 100 or so other ethnic groups, including Kazakh, Kyrgyr, Tajik, Tartar and Turkmen. Most of the ethnic minorities live in or around Tashkent and other urban centres. Some 43 per cent of the population were below age 16 in 1994, and 8 per cent were past working age. Since not all people of working age are employed, the actual wage dependency ratio was high, estimated as 1.6 dependants for each worker.[35]

In 1995 Uzbekistan's TFR was estimated as 4.1 children per woman, but the 1996 Demographic and Health Survey (DHS) found a much smaller TFR of only 3.3.[36] Since the DHS approach to demographic data collection tends to be more comprehensive than other sources, the lower estimate, or somewhere near it, is more likely. In Tashkent the TFR was as low as 2.3 children per woman, while it was highest in Namanganskaya, Ferghanskaya and Andizhanskaya provinces.[37] One factor contributing to lower fertility is fewer marriages in recent years because of uncertain economic conditions, but because of the young age structure, there is considerable population growth momentum.[38]

By world standards, mortality appears relatively low in Uzbekistan, and considerably better than in Mongolia. It must be noted, however, that, as in Mongolia, the method of calculation of the IMR is not strictly comparable with that used in non-Soviet countries, since the Soviet definition of live birth excludes those dying in the first seven days after delivery. This could be as many as 25 per cent of all infant deaths. The reported IMR in 1994 was 28 deaths per 1000 live births. It ranged from a maximum of 35 in one of the poorest provinces, Karakalpakstan, to 24 in Syrdarya, with Tashkent City a little higher, at 26.[39] Interestingly, the IMR was generally higher in urban areas than in the countryside in all provinces, with an overall rate of 29 per 1000 in urban areas compared with 28 in rural areas. Life expectancy at birth in 1994 was 68 for men and 73 for women.[40]

This combination of reasonably high fertility and relatively low mortality has contributed to a vigorous population growth rate, estimated as 2.2 per cent per annum in 1995. This was a substantial decline from much higher rates of 2.7 per cent in 1985 and 2.5 per cent in 1990. A further decline to around 1.8 per cent per annum is expected by 2000.[41] The disintegration of the USSR resulted in significant emigration from Uzbekistan, peaking at almost 100,000 per annum in the late 1980s. Most emigrants are members of minority groups, such as Germans, Russians, Ukrainians or Jews, returning to ethnic or religious homelands. This movement has constituted a serious 'brain-drain', since the majority of emigrants are well-educated professionals and managers, who must be replaced.[42] Despite the negative migration balance, declining fertility and slowing population growth rate, Uzbekistan's total population is still expected to reach 35 million by 2015.[43]

Health

Uzbekistan has a well-developed, Soviet-style health care system, established while it was a part of the USSR. This system is similar to that adopted by Mongolia, but was more advanced with much greater capacity to serve the needs of the population. Like the Mongolian system it is based on a hierarchy of public medical services, ranging from paramedical and obstetric aid posts up to specialized centres capable of offering complex surgical procedures. Much greater investment in Uzbekistan's health sector, however, has resulted in health service indicators which, until recently, compared favourably with neighbouring countries and with some of the most developed countries. In the early 1990s Uzbekistan's ratio of 3.5 doctors per 1000 people was almost three times that of the UK and almost 50 per cent better than that of the USA. The ratio of 9.4 hospital beds per thousand people was 50 per cent higher than that of the UK and about 80 per cent higher than in the USA.[44] Until the early 1990s health care in Uzbekistan was available to all without charge.

Even so, progress in health was uneven and the morbidity pattern comprised high levels of both infectious and NCDs, even before separation from the USSR led to a decline in health funding. In particular, there were high levels of anaemia, cancer, cardiovascular diseases and infectious diseases associated with poor water and sanitation, including typhoid and hepatitis. More recently there have been increasing incidences of polio, measles and diphtheria because of shortages of supplies of vaccines. Children compose 70–75 per cent of hepatitis cases.[45] Information on the prevalence of STDs in Uzbekistan was not available at the time of writing, but they are likely to be less well treated than in the past, in view of the deteriorating health facilities.

This pattern of uneven progress in health is largely a product of the nature of development and industrialization in Uzbekistan rather than any lack of investment in the health sector. The main causes are thus external factors, with sociological factors playing a lesser role. Three main causes of uneven progress can be identified: first, environmental contamination; second, urbanization and increased lifestyle risk factors; and third, as in Mongolia, the health care system's emphasis on curative rather than preventive medicine.

Environmental contamination

Uzbekistan's disease pattern is closely associated with geographical location. Infectious diseases and diseases of the alimentary tract are more common in rural areas, while cardiovascular, blood and respiratory diseases and malignant tumours predominate in urban areas.[46] Morbidity rates in the contaminated Aral Sea region were 50–70 per cent higher than the national average in the 1990s; medical surveys revealed that around 70 per cent of the population had a major illness. Of these 43 per cent were anaemic, 21 per cent had cardiovascular disease and 13 per cent a kidney disease.[47]

Much of this is due to chemical contamination. Although the use of fertilizers and pesticides has been scaled back in recent years, contaminants from former activities remain. Up to 30 per cent of the potassium and nitrate fertilizers not absorbed by plants were washed into ground waters and surrounding soils. Pesticide residues in ground water and soil such as DDT exceeded acceptable levels by two or three times, not only in the Aral region but also in Ferghana, Samarkand and some other provinces. Samarkand had ten times more than the internationally acceptable levels of zinc and six times the acceptable levels of arsenic pollution in 1993.[48]

Pollution of the Aral Sea and other waterways contributes to infectious diseases such as hepatitis, typhoid and diarrhoeal diseases. Rivers are contaminated with waste from cattle breeding and industrial enterprises. Polluted water from some metallurgical, chemical and oil industries is discharged into reservoirs, without purification. The Uzbekistan Research Institute of Sanitation, Hygiene and Occupational Disease estimates that 79 per cent of all acute intestinal infections and 85 per cent of all water-borne diseases occurred in rural regions without a proper water supply, where residents are obliged to use canals and ponds for drinking and washing. The provision of potable water in rural areas has been prioritized since 1990, but it is estimated that 50 per cent of rural water and about one-third of that supplied to urban centres is still unsafe.[49]

Environmental contamination on a very large scale is thus an important cause of sickness in Uzbekistan. Whereas lack of knowledge of the nature of pollutants was a worldwide cause of contamination in the past, Uzbekistan was subject to a disproportionate share of contamination because of its function in the former Russian and Soviet Empires as a cotton growing area. In addition, industrial workers were exploited without regard to their environment, safety or quality of life, and industrial waste was disposed of as cheaply as possible without regard for the environmental consequences. Thus Uzbekistan's role as a peripheral economy exacerbated its exposure to contamination and had a severely negative impact on population health.

Increased lifestyle risk factors

As well as environmental contamination, there has been an increase in lifestyle risk factors in Uzbekistan as a consequence of urbanization. This too has been exacerbated by marginalization within the Soviet sphere of influence. Of particular concern is poor nutrition. Traditionally the Uzbek diet comprised a high proportion of animal products, which contribute to high levels of cardiovascular disease, although the diet was generally more varied than that of Mongolians. Recent nutrition statistics indicate that consumption of meat products in Uzbekistan has declined, and there also are shortfalls in the consumption of dairy products, eggs and other protein sources, down to around half the recommended WHO intakes.[50] Whereas this may not be a serious concern for older people and adults living sedentary lifestyles in urban areas, it is severely affecting the health of children and women of reproductive age. Deficiency diseases include high levels of anaemia, especially among women and children, and iodine and vitamin A deficiency. Iodized salt and other products fortified with iodine are not generally available. In 1991 a sample of children aged 3–7 years were found to be consuming only 83 per cent of the recommended calorie intake, and only 40 per cent of the recommended protein.[51] Around 60 per cent of women of child bearing age were anaemic in 1995.[52]

Food intake varies considerably between regions, with average caloric intake in the cattle breeding areas of Syrdarya as much as 65 per cent higher than in some of the cotton provinces, such as Karakalpakstan. While there appears to be an increasing prevalence of low food intake in rural areas, there is evidence of an increasing prevalence of obesity among older and urban populations. Within Uzbekistan this is generally attributed to a high intake of carbohydrates, especially bread, and inadequate consumption of meat and dairy produce.[53] In fact, it is now generally agreed by nutritionists that obesity is unlikely to be due primarily to high levels of consumption of carbohydrates. A more likely cause is fats and oils and other high calorie foods which are eaten with the bread, which may not be reported in nutrition surveys unless respondents are prompted or observed closely while eating. For example, in 1997 Goscomprognozstat officials expressed concern to one of the authors of this book that recent household surveys had yielded estimates of food intake as low as 1800 calories per day, which are implausible because they are too low to keep adults alive in the long term. Clearly nutrition estimates from that survey, which were based on respondent recall, lacked precision.

It appears that Uzbekistan is developing the increasingly common pattern of over-nutrition of some adults and under-nutrition of women and children. This points to a need to increase allocation of proteins and fats to children and iron-rich foods to women. A reduced intake of animal products need not have a deleterious effect on the nutrition of the rest of the adult population if they have an adequate intake of vitamins from fruit and vegetables. Rather, it could bring benefits in the form of a reduction in obesity and cardiovascular disease.

It is arguable that the main limitation to contemporary Uzbek diets is a lack of fresh fruit and vegetables rather than the scarcity of animal products. Post-independence strategies to convert a million hectares of cotton land to cultivation of grains, fruit and vegetables have increased the supply of these products.[54] However, nutritional education is needed to promote healthy eating habits. There is still a heavy reliance on bread supplemented with high fat meat stews, tea and sugar, while fresh fruit and vegetables are relatively expensive and difficult to obtain. In 1997 fresh fruit and vegetables were little in evidence in Tashkent supermarkets, while much of the produce sold in the bazaars had travelled long distances and was no longer fresh by the time it reached the point of sale. Surprisingly, good quality bananas imported from Colombia were available for about US$0.70 each on street stalls, whereas a loaf of bread cost US$0.30.

The stress of marginalization and urban living has contributed to ill health and an increasing incidence of NCDs by encouraging the adoption of other high-risk lifestyle habits. In the past alcohol consumption and tobacco smoking have contributed to higher rates of cardiovascular disease and malignant neoplasm among urban populations. Ironically, one beneficial consequence of harsher economic conditions has been a reduction in the consumption of alcohol and tobacco. In 1985 absolute alcohol consumption was estimated at a very high 4.6 litres per adult per year, but this declined to 3.4 litres in 1990, and 1.7 litres per adult by 1994, largely as a result of the increased cost of living and declining incomes following independence. The rate of chronic alcoholism declined by 29 per cent between 1990 and 1994, and alcohol related psychiatric disorders by 3 per cent.[55] Price increases affected tobacco smoking even more, from 1.7 kg per adult to only 0.1 kg per adult. The resurgence of Islam is also contributing to a reduction in the consumption of alcohol and tobacco, especially among more traditional social groups.

Even so, alcoholism remains a matter of concern for health authorities, as in a number of former members of the USSR, including Russia, and in Mongolia. Beer, wines and spirits are freely available in Tashkent at prices easily affordable to those who are benefiting most from the transition to a market economy. At the same time the stress of a changing mode of life and economic insecurity is affecting many urban dwellers and encourages self-destructive behavioural patterns.

Inappropriate health system

The third major cause of uneven progress in health in Uzbekistan is the nature of the health care system. As in Mongolia, the health system has emphasized curative medicine and specialized care while neglecting preventive medicine, especially primary health care and health education. This reflects the Soviet influence in Uzbek health care, and has led to concerns that the relatively lavish health funding of the past was managed inefficiently.[56] Investment in public health measures could have brought greater gains in health. Loss of Moscow funding following separation from the USSR led to a reduction in the number of hospital beds by 16 per cent between 1990 and 1994.[57] At the same time efforts were made to increase the availability of health funding, including introducing fees for some medicines, reducing the average duration of a hospital stay and introducing a health insurance scheme.[58] Since these measures were associated with a general running down of the health system with no corresponding increase in expenditure on preventive medicine, general health also deteriorated. Overall, sickness rates increased by about 12 per cent between 1991 and 1995. The main cause of death in the period 1990–1993 was blood disease, including sepsis, which may have been treatable by a better hospital system, but which could certainly have been reduced by public health measures.

The cause of mismanagement in the health sector does not seem to be lack of understanding by health authorities of the need to control infectious disease. In 1995 there were 253 sanitation and epidemiological centres, 221 anti-infection stations, 132 health centres responsible for inspecting sanitary conditions, water supply and nutrition of the population, and 15 HIV/AIDS testing units.[59] However, many of these centres were staffed by paramedics with only secondary education, who lack the skills to provide a wide range of services. Although sophisticated diagnostic facilities are available in some health facilities, many others lack clinical and diagnostic equipment, so that diseases may go undetected in their initial stages, when they would be most responsive to treatment.

There is also a tendency to use facilities inefficiently. For example, primary care centres are often overloaded with patients seeking emergency care. A survey of medical doctors found that, on average, only 5 per cent of their time was devoted to preventive medicine.[60]

As in Mongolia, a weakness of Uzbekistan's health system has been its limited involvement with local communities. This has become a key strategy in the worldwide primary health care initiative, but seems to have been regarded as incompatible with socialist systems. A positive sign is the 1994 government initiative to recognize mahalla community organizations as a mechanism to distribute assistance to poor families. These organizations, which have an established record of coordinating community activities, could be further utilized in primary health care initiatives.

Another major weakness in Uzbekistan's health system, as in Mongolia, has been the poor quality of maternal and child health care. In particular monitoring of pregnant mothers and young children has been neglected, resulting in a high prevalence of anaemia, low birth weight, and poor growth attainment. Following independence there was a substantial decline in the proportions of eligible children immunized against the main infectious childhood diseases. For example, immunization coverage rates for diphtheria, polio and pertussis (whooping cough) almost halved between 1991 and 1993. In 1994 immunization coverage for the above diseases plus tetanus and mumps was below 40 per cent of each eligible age group, with only measles immunization exceeding 60 per cent.[61]

As in some other socialist countries, the provision of family planning services has been neglected. As a consequence births are frequently too closely spaced, which contributes to depletion of maternal health, anaemia and maternal mortality, and also to sibling competition for family resources.[62] Although an estimated 56 per cent of women aged 15–49 use family planning, contraceptive choice has been limited, with IUDs, which are available free of charge, the main method available.[63] Very few use hormonal contraceptives because of unreliable supplies, while lack of access to, or misuse of, alternative methods, has led to widespread use of abortion as an alternative to birth control.[64] In the 1980s the government promoted family planning, but the emphasis was on limiting family size rather than on more acceptable health objectives. In the post-independence period new policies to promote the health of women of reproductive age reduced the maternal mortality rate from 73 per 100,000 live births in 1990 to 37 in 1994,[65] and some sources have suggested to as low as 17.[66]

Despite some progress, and an almost doubling of government funding for primary care between 1993 and 1995 to 35 per cent of the health budget, many structural problems remain in the health care system. One of the most important constraints derives from the transition to a market economy. The health profession is becoming increasingly less attractive to school leavers as the market economic structure develops. Salaries in the health sector, as well as other social sectors, have now fallen below the national mean, reducing incentives to participate.[67] The health sector, along with other social sectors such as education, is thus being disadvantaged rather than improved by the nature of Uzbekistan's economic growth.

SUMMARY

The peripheral locations of Mongolia and Uzbekistan have impeded progress in health. Both countries adopted a Soviet-style health system, which emphasized curative rather than preventive medicine. Even when this system was highly developed, as in Uzbekistan, it was still unable to achieve generally good population health because it did little to address the underlying causes of ill health. At the same time, industrialization, urbanization and changes in lifestyles increased environmental contamination, which impacted negatively on the health of large percentages of their populations.

In both countries the initial phases, at least, of the transition to a market economy produced deteriorating health indicators. Reductions in health expenditure led to sharp increases in the prevalence of illness in both countries, primarily because the capacity to cure illness was reduced, while preventive medicine continued to be under-emphasized. It is likely to be some years before either country is capable of achieving the socioeconomic and health system management changes necessary to complete a health transition to a pattern of long life expectancies and a low incidence of infectious disease.

Uneven progress in health and failure to effect a complete health transition, as exhibited by these two landlocked socialist countries on the periphery of the former USSR, can also be observed in the totally different context of Pacific democracies. A number of small Pacific Island states have experienced uneven progress in health. This has occurred despite considerable natural advantages in terms of environment and lifestyle options as compared with the two socialist countries discussed above. The next chapter considers health in the Pacific region, with special attention to the Marshall Islands. It begins with a brief history of Pacific population, health and disease patterns at the time of first contact with Europeans. It then examines changes in health and lifestyles in the Marshall Islands, demonstrating that the impact of a peripheral location on external and sociological determinants of health can limit progress, even in what might be considered a very favourable health environment.

Chapter 7

Uneven Progress in Health in the Pacific Region

The Pacific provides an agreeable living environment compared with the harsher settings of Central and East Asia. Warm climates enable people to live with only rudimentary shelter and clothing. Fish are abundant and readily caught in the shallow lagoons and coral reefs which surround most islands. Naturally growing coconuts are ubiquitous, and most islands also grow nutritious fruit such as banana, papaya and breadfruit. The larger islands have fertile soils which support the cultivation of root crops and vegetables. Although traditional Pacific populations needed sophisticated survival skills to enable them to exploit their environment, and to cope with occasional major hazards such as destructive cyclones and severe droughts, for the most part they were able to live comfortably with comparatively little hardship. Such a lifestyle is representative of the pre-colonial contact era. On remote islands it is possible to experience such a lifestyle, but this is increasingly unusual.

Except in the malarial areas of Melanesia, island populations were relatively free of infectious diseases before first contact. The pursuit of traditional lifestyles in the Pacific is generally thought to be a healthy activity, providing a balanced diet and the exercise of gathering it. Aside from deaths in infancy and childbirth, the most common causes of death were injury and drowning, but otherwise there were likely to have been few threats to health other than periodic food shortages.

The dispersal of the islands across vast expanses of ocean and the difficulty of travel between them militated against the emergence of far reaching indigenous empires based on territory, such as those of Central and East Asia. Even so, some Pacific countries were drawn into relationships of dependency with dominant powers as a consequence of globalization. As in Mongolia and Uzbekistan, globalization has affected Pacific health and lifestyles, although in different ways. This chapter considers how global forces have shaped population and health in the Marshall Islands, with some reference to other Pacific states. It shows how people accustomed to life in a small island culture in a congenial Pacific environment have responded to modernization. Although there are some similarities with Mongolia and Uzbekistan, in other ways their experiences and responses more closely resemble those of economically marginalized groups within the world's most developed societies. Most notably, in the Marshall Islands uneven progress in health has been due to sociological factors as much as to external factors. The economic and social pressures of contact with the developed countries on the Pacific Rim, especially with the USA, have led many Marshallese to choose high-risk lifestyle habits, even though other healthier options could have been selected.

POPULATION AND HEALTH PRIOR TO THE SECOND WORLD WAR

Little is known about Pacific population numbers before European contact, but it is evident that initial contact with the outside world brought substantial depopulation by introducing infectious diseases. The Spanish explorers of the 16th century had little direct contact with the people, although they may have left behind rats and pigs. Whalers, traders and missionaries who followed them had more contact with the local people, and brought devastating epidemics of infectious diseases to much of the Pacific. Illnesses which Europeans regarded as minor, such as the common cold, produced serious illness and death in Pacific populations which had not previously been exposed to them and thus had no natural immunity. More serious illnesses such as measles, pneumonia, tuberculosis, diphtheria, scarlet fever, typhoid and cholera caused huge mortality rates.[1]

In the Marshall Islands, where whaling activities were limited, the first significant contact with traders and planters in the mid-19th century brought serious disease and depopulation. It is difficult to estimate the number of deaths, since early population estimates vary.

In the 1890s Finsch, a German ethnologist, considered that previous estimates of a total population of 10,000 were too high. Interestingly, he found the Marshallese to be apparently unconcerned with population numbers and reported that several island 'kings' did not know how many subjects they had. In his view the:

> *native population had diminished and died out when they came into close contact with whites ... the Marshallese are not a long lived race ... women fade quickly ... men rapidly come to the stage of senility ... unions between whites and natives generally are unfulfilled.*[2]

This last observation seems odd in view of the extensive intermingling of foreign blood with Marshallese; some contemporary Marshallese families carry the names of the early traders, such as de Brum and Capelle.

Although disease clearly did have a major impact on the Marshallese population during the 19th century, Finsch makes little mention of infectious disease other than to observe that syphilis had been introduced 'a long time ago' and 'influenza was often fatal'.[3] Generally he places more importance on other factors. For example, Rongelap and Rongerik had 80 and 120 inhabitants respectively in the middle of the century but had dwindled to 10 and 18 by the late 1880s, along with abandoned huts for 100: 'the majority had been driven to the South while on a general canoe voyage and had perished'.[4]

According to Finsch, the Marshallese in the 1890s were 'smaller and weaker in appearance than the Gilbert Islanders ... with widespread skin eruptions and ringworm'. He cites various descriptions of the Marshallese character by passing observers, which range from idyllic 'noble savage' images to his own portrayal of a more worldly people, which still rings true today. He also emphasizes their quiet and subdued nature and their submission to nobility. Although describing them as generally a very peaceful people, he mentions various incidences of attacks on ships. Interestingly, he wrote that drunkenness was relatively uncommon 'since only the chiefs could afford it, although they were very fond of it', yet locally brewed toddy was readily available to all.

Following the First World War, most of Micronesia was mandated to Japan and became part of the Japanese East Asia Co-

Prosperity Sphere, as described in Chapter 4. Intensive economic activity during this period drew the islands further into the global economy than had previous contact with foreign powers. Even so, there was little population increase, and the 1920 total was still only about 9800.[5] Depopulation resulting from contact with the outside world was an established trend well before the Japanese period, and there is evidence that the decline had actually halted by 1914. Japanese navy doctors provided health care for sick and injured Micronesians, and in 1922 government hospitals were established at various sites in Micronesia, including Jaluit in the Marshall Islands.[6]

Other health-related activities introduced by the Japanese included compulsory immunization programmes, and training of indigenous women to educate villagers in sanitation and the improvement of personal hygiene. This represented an early concern with preventive medicine, and it seems that indigenous populations might have flourished under the Japanese regime.

The war brought extreme hardship to the Japanese and to the Micronesians they employed. Japanese encamped on isolated atolls found their supplies cut off and were bombarded by the American offensive. In the Marshall Islands they relied increasingly on the local people for their survival. A Maloelap informant who had worked for the Japanese during the war described extreme hardship, food shortages and the Japanese insistence that the Marshallese remain loyal to them. Just before the Americans arrived the people of the main island in Maloelap atoll, Taroa, fled across the lagoon to a smaller island where they may not have survived long but for being taken on board an American naval vessel. He said that although they had been told by the Japanese to fear the Americans, the people soon became very grateful to them because they cared for the refugees with food and medical treatment.

POPULATION PATTERNS IN THE POST-WAR PERIOD

By the end of the Second World War the Marshallese population growth rate was still very slow, or at times negative, and the population had incremented only gradually to around 10,000 or 11,000. The dramatic socioeconomic change after the war, which occurred as a result of the American presence, led to escalating population growth rates. The average annual growth rate reached

4.1 per cent per annum in the period 1967–73, declined slightly in the following years and then peaked at 4.2 per cent per annum in 1980–88.[7]

Marshallese censuses exclude Americans stationed at the military base, so the majority of the population are Marshalls-born, with small percentages from elsewhere in the Pacific or born in the USA. Since there was little permanent international migration prior to 1988, the Marshall Islands appeared to have one of the highest population growth rates in the world in the period 1980–1988, 4.2 per cent per annum. In 1988 the total population census count was 43,400, and the 1988 growth rate had the capacity to double the population every 20 years. The cause of this extremely high growth rate was very high fertility, coupled with moderate mortality. The total fertility rate had been more than seven births per woman since the 1960s, and may have been as high as 8.7 children er woman in 1964–1968.[8]

Even allowing for a small decline in the growth rate, a population of close to 60,000 would have been expected in 1999. However, the 1999 census count was only 50,840 and the growth rate was said to have fallen dramatically to only 1.5 per cent.[9] Fertility reductions in the contemporary world are normally attributed to increases in family planning uptake. Family planning uptake in the Marshall Islands in 1994 implied a total fertility rate of around five children per woman, and there is no evidence to suggest that it has increased markedly since. The 1999 census report attributes the apparent slowing in the overall population growth rate between 1988 and 1999 to a substantial increase in emigration. However, as the Marshall Islands did not keep statistics on emigration at the time of writing it is not clear if this is so, or whether the apparent slowing of the population growth rate can be attributed to the difficulty of counting several thousand people scattered across many small islets and islands.

Despite substantial US investment in health since the war years, life expectancy at birth has increased quite slowly. According to the 1988 census it was only 60 years for men and 63 years for women, and there is no indication that it has improved significantly since then.[10] There are two main reasons for this comparatively small improvement in life expectancy. First is that the IMR was slow to decline, at least until recently. By 1988 it was still as high as 63 infant deaths per 1000 live births, even though it had declined from pre-war days.[11] The Ministry of Health and Environment (MOHE) estimated that infant mortality fell to 27 per 1000 for 1996. However, as the total number of infant deaths in the Marshall Islands each year since 1990 has ranged only from 40 to 58,[12] the IMR is affected by chance fluctuations and it is too soon to discern a long-term trend. The second reason for relatively low life expectancy is that gains in child survival and a reduction of infectious disease have been offset by high prevalence of NCDs in adulthood. This has contributed to a comparatively high incidence of mortality among adults who have not yet reached their 60s and 70s.

The pattern of very high fertility and high adult mortality has resulted in an age structure heavily weighted towards the youngest age groups. In 1988 51 per cent of the population was aged under 15 years and the ratio of working age to non-working age population was almost 1.2.[13] Although this ratio may have improved slightly with recent fertility declines, many people of working age are not in the labour force, while perhaps 20 per cent of the labour force are unemployed. The young age structure thus constitutes a significant economic burden.

CHANGING LIFESTYLES IN THE POST-WAR PERIOD

This marked change in the Marshallese population growth rate was a consequence of changes in living conditions after the Second World War. The US administration following 1945 heralded a major lifestyle change for those Micronesians who had been involved in the Pacific War. The extent of US influence varied between countries. Most notably this related to the extent to which the USA established military installations in the region. As sites of US military bases, Guam and the Marshall Islands were most exposed to American influences. FSM had a much lower priority among US strategists, which partially explains why these islands, especially Yap, have maintained their traditional culture to a greater extent than other parts of Micronesia. Although it had only a token US military presence, Palau's 1980s attempts to introduce a constitution with explicit anti-nuclear clauses highlighted its potential for US military use.[14] While the USA never fully admitted that Palau was earmarked as a nuclear base, it was the obvious fallback position should a withdrawal from the Philippines be necessary. This intensified interaction with the USA, and facilitated a stronger American influence on Palauan lifestyles.

Eventually US involvement in the Marshall Islands became so extensive that it supported a dramatic increase in urbanization and the abandonment of traditional lifestyles by almost 70 per cent of the population,[15] a level similar to those of many developed countries. However, since Marshallese urbanization was founded on US military activity and US economic assistance rather than on indigenous economic activity, the Marshallese people were in a sense peripheral, and had only limited capacity to determine events within their own country. The main motivation for moving to urban areas was the attraction of 'the bright lights', that is, to adopt a more stimulating lifestyle, and also to have ready access to store-bought food. They were able to do this because more money was circulating in the economy, but there were few opportunities for employment in the modern sector, while economic benefits from the American presence were largely controlled by traditional leaders. As a consequence, only a handful of people were actively involved in the nation's development, while the majority were marginalized, in a way similar to that of some other minority groups, such as Native Americans and the Australian Aboriginal people. As is common with these groups, many urban Marshallese also tended to slip into unhealthy lifestyles. They were removed from the means to practise subsistence agriculture, living in crowded and unsanitary conditions, frequently poor, having access to an inadequate diet and little or no opportunity to exercise, and drinking alcohol and smoking tobacco to relieve stress and boredom. Although easier access to food and more sedentary lifestyles supported rapid population increase, it also produced a raft of health problems related to diet and lifestyle habits.

CHANGES IN NUTRITION

The adoption of a diet based primarily on white rice, refined white flour, sugar and high-fat meats has been associated with a dramatic increase in NCDs, many related to people being overweight and obesity. Similar patterns can be found or are developing elsewhere in the Pacific, including Fiji, Nauru and Samoa. Early-onset diabetes has become the most important and widespread health problem in the Marshall Islands.

The establishment of coconut oil and copra industries in the 1860s led to the importation of tobacco, weapons, spirits, cotton goods, rice and ships biscuits.[16] As the coconut industries also provided income earning opportunities for the local population, this was probably the time when rice began to be a significant item in the diets of some Marshallese. In 1906 another German observer, Kramer, remarked on the paucity of the Marshallese diet, stating that hens and pigs were generally absent and sea birds rare and difficult to catch, while there was only one land bird, the fruit dove. The main proteins were fish, crayfish and turtle. He also reported that the incidence of fish poisoning was much higher than in Samoa. He attributed this to poor handling and preparation, although fish poisoning is now recognized as being caused by the development of toxins within the fish themselves, as a consequence of events such as feeding on coral. Kramer gives a detailed description of common methods of preserving the starch staples arrowroot and pandanus,[17] a practice which has become less common today.

There is no evidence that Micronesian diets changed significantly during the Japanese period. The Japanese preference for rice as a staple was nothing new in Micronesia, since by then rice had already become an established part of Micronesian diets. The Japanese generally avoided local foods and keep strictly to a diet of imported Japanese food. They were alleged to ignore even sashimi prepared from raw local fish, preferring to eat imported fish from cans.[18] Except for rice, imported Japanese foods were very expensive, and generally only elite Pacific islanders could afford to purchase them. The mandate charter prohibited the sale or supply of spirits to the indigenous population, but since Micronesians traditionally manufactured alcoholic toddies, they were still able to become intoxicated when they wished. Consequently, drunkenness was said to be the main cause of arrest during the Japanese era. By 1938, however, the rules were relaxed and chiefs were occasionally invited to drink the Emperor's health in sake.[19]

Nutrition surveys carried out in 1951 and 1991 provide detailed information on dietary patterns and change in the Marshall Islands in the post-war period. A comparison of the results of the nutrition surveys sheds some light on the rate of dietary change and its progressive impact on health. The nutrition survey of 1951 showed that Marshallese were still consuming 'traditional foods' but becoming increasingly dependent on imported foods. The foods listed as the Marshallese diet, and for which there were Marshallese words, were various dishes prepared from pandanus, breadfruit, coconut, heart of palm, banana, various fish, arrowroot, chicken, pork, soy sauce, sugar, rice, lobster, eel, pumpkin, coconut, crab, whale, turtle, porpoise, octopus, squid and other marine creatures, and a range of sea birds.[20]

Imported food was purchased from trade stores. Salary scales in 1951 were described as low, and food prices high compared with the USA. When asked whether they could fish to augment their food supply, Marshallese respondents said they did not have time to fish so had to depend on imported canned food. It was felt that obtaining enough food was an economic hardship, especially canned meats, canned fish and evaporated milk. Even so, store-keepers reported that the demand for imported foods always exceeded supply.[21] Locally baked bread and fried doughnuts were already very popular by 1951 and it was also reported that the Marshallese added large amounts of sugar to their tea.

The 1951 nutrition survey assessed the diets of Marshallese in all age groups as consistently very deficient in calories, vitamins and minerals, and especially in leafy vegetables, milk, fruit, meat, eggs and beans.[22] Although Marshallese children aged 1–3 years were, on average, the same weight as American children of similar age, those aged 4–6 years were only 71 per cent of the weight of comparable American children.[23] Forty years later the 1991 survey found that around 20 per cent of pre-schoolers were underweight and 24 per cent of children aged up to seven years were stunted (significantly below normal height for age). At ages 7–14 years 35 per cent of children were stunted.[24]

In contrast to the pattern for children, which was dominated by significant levels of underweight and stunting, the striking feature of adult growth attainment was the high level of obesity. In 1991 31 per cent of 700 non-pregnant Marshallese women aged 15–49 years were classified as obese, and another 30 per cent as overweight.[25] Twenty per cent of adolescent girls surveyed were overweight, and obesity became more prevalent as age increased. Obesity in adults was associated with high rates of diabetes, hypertension, and cardiac and osteopathic problems, and premature death.

As early as 1974 a survey of 375 adult Marshallese found that 26 per cent had abnormally high blood sugar levels, although the prevalence of retinopathy and vascular disease among them was low.[26] In 1985 30 per cent of surveyed Majuro women aged 40–59 were diabetic.[27] Although diabetes is less frequently the immediate cause of death compared with some other conditions, it is a common underlying cause of death. Cardiovascular disease, hypertension and cancer also affect unusually large percentages of Marshallese, and at younger ages than are typical in other countries.

Despite concern over diseases related to obesity, it is difficult to find recent estimates of the prevalence of diabetes in the Marshall Islands. Majuro hospital statistics for 1996 indicate that 60 of 126 people screened were positive, but there is no indication of the basis for selection of candidates for screening.[28] It is thought that as many as 30 per cent of adults may have diabetes,[29] but it is impossible to estimate age specific prevalence rates, and only notifiable diseases are reported in the health statistics abstracts.[30]

FACTORS SUPPORTING OBESITY AND UNHEALTHY LIFESTYLES IN THE PACIFIC

The aspects of contemporary Marshallese lifestyles most related to the high prevalence of NCDs are consumption of a high-sugar, high-fat, low-fibre diet, alcohol consumption, smoking and lack of physical exercise. With the exception of smoking, those factors tend to act on health initially by contributing to being overweight and obesity, which are risk factors for a number of NCDs. Moreover, these energy-dense fatty and sugary foods tend to be deficient in some essential vitamins and minerals.[31] In the Marshall Islands, as elsewhere, the most important diseases associated with excess body weight and obesity are coronary heart disease, cerebrovascular disease, various cancers, diabetes mellitus, gallstones, dental caries, gastrointestinal disorders and various bone and joint disorders.[32]

The high prevalence of obesity in the Marshall Islands, as in some other societies, is in part supported by social factors. Cultural fattening processes have been documented in countries as diverse as Italy, Cameroon, Nigeria and Nauru.[33] Obesity also has long been regarded as a symbol of high social status and prosperity in much of the Pacific, and this view is also held in the Marshall Islands. None the less, historical evidence from early travellers and early photographic records indicate that obesity has become more common since the arrival of Europeans. In Samoa obesity is viewed as desirable and healthy in people of high status, but less so in commoners.[34] Data for Nauru, Samoa and Niue indicate that the prevalence of obesity is increasing, and there are more cases at younger ages. The prevalence also appears to be higher among women than among men in most Pacific countries. In Samoa in 1991 obesity was significantly higher among those in sedentary occupations. A reflection of this is that for women especially, the odds of being obese increased with education.[35]

One possible explanation for the high prevalence of being overweight and obesity among Pacific populations is the 'thrifty gene'. It is argued that a particular genotype confers a survival advantage where marked fluctuations in food availability exist, such as in the traditional Pacific lifestyle. People with this gene, including Pacific and Australian Aboriginal populations, are very efficient at storing nutrients in the form of fat reserves which can be burned up when food intake decreases. They are thus more able to store nutrients during the 'feast' periods and more able to survive 'famine' situations. Since food availability tends to be more uniform in urban environments and there are no 'famines', people with this genotype store too much fat when exposed to a high-fat, high-sugar, low-fibre Western diet. If they never encounter periods of food shortage the fat reserves simply accumulate, and so they tend to become obese.[36]

The most prevalent obesity-related disease, diabetes, is considerably higher among some Pacific populations than among Caucasian groups. However, although obesity is the most important factor in the aetiology of diabetes, not all obese people become diabetic and not all diabetics are obese. A Nauru study found the prevalence of diabetes was 2–4 times as high in obese Nauruans as in lean Nauruans, and 72 per cent of diabetic Nauruans had a family history of diabetes. On the other hand, diabetics in Papua New Guinea and Fijian Indians are not usually obese, while the relationship of diabetes and obesity is inconsistent in Samoa. It is therefore argued that the importance of obesity in precipitating early onset diabetes may be more important for some groups than for others.[37]

Pollock argues that there is a sound physiological basis for fattening when there is no food security, as only women who have stored sufficient reserves of fat have the capacity to nourish a fetus during periods of food scarcity. This is the basis of puberty fattening in Nauru and the Marshall Islands, which produces a side effect of lightening of the skin as a consequence of long and inactive sojourns in fattening houses. Pollock considers that this has contributed to the appreciation of fatness as a sign of social status and beauty in Nauru, which has parallels elsewhere in the Pacific. In addition to this she strongly defends the cultural valuing of fatness, and argues that epidemiologists have taken too narrow a view in attributing high prevalence of diabetes primarily to obesity and by defining obesity itself as a disease.[38]

The issue of concern, however, should be health risk factors, rather than obesity per se. It is clear that dramatic changes in the composition of diets in Pacific countries have contributed to the increasing prevalence of diabetes, along with improvements in diagnosis and increased survival as a result of better management. Whether or not it is the obesity itself, or other factors such as the addition of stress, metabolic changes resulting from new diets, or any other factors, is less important than the issue of how to minimize risk factors. Even if obesity were not associated with increased health risks in the past, it certainly is today, and hence high prevalence of obesity has become a matter for serious concern.

In the Marshall Islands the substitution of rice, tinned meat, fish and vegetables, sugar, tea, soft drinks and alcohol for a tradi-tional diet is clearly a leading factor contributing to overweight and to diabetes. These low-fibre, high-fat, high-sugar diets also generate other conditions which are contributory factors to diabetes, including pancreatitis (as a consequence of high alcohol consumption) and haemochromatosis (from too much iron). Other possible contributory causes of diabetes are deficiencies of potas-sium, protein, chromium, zinc and pyridoxine, consumption of cassava and infrequent feeding or gorging.[39]

Reduced opportunities for exercise in mechanized and urban-ized societies are also important. 'Outboard motors have replaced canoe paddles, cars have replaced walking, and tractors have replaced hoes. Buying food requires less energy than producing it'.[40] Exercise may reduce the risk of diabetes by improving glucose tolerance, or by producing a leaner body. The Diabetes Reversal Program conducted by Canvasback Missions was able to achieve dramatic lowering of blood sugar in Marshallese diabetic patients within a few days by placing them on a high-fibre diet and an exercise regime.[41]

Another factor which contributes to obesity and may also be directly associated with diabetes is stress. As discussed in Chapter

3, it is widely recognized that people who have no ready outlet for stress have an increased risk of developing health problems. Urban Marshallese not only tend to be sedentary but are also likely to be stressed by a variety of social and economic factors, as will be shown in Chapter 9. One complication of obesity and diabetes which is also affected by stress is cardiovascular disease, a leading cause of death in the Marshall Islands. Cardiovascular diseases include coronary heart disease, cerebrovascular disease and hypertension. Cardiovascular risk factors include high levels of cholesterol and triglycerides, which are associated with obesity.[42] In some Pacific communities the incidence of cardiovascular disease is relatively low given the levels of obesity that exist, and it has been hypothesized that there is a significant time lag between the development of obesity and diabetes and the appearance of cardiovascular diseases and atherosclerosis.[43] The trend towards increasingly early onset of obesity and diabetes in the Marshall Islands may therefore be a factor contributing to the high prevalence of cardiovascular diseases.

The impact of retailers' preferences on Marshallese diets, and also those of other Pacific populations, must also be considered. In the Pacific, nutrition has tended to be viewed mainly as a health issue and little attention has been paid to the availability of food and to linking nutrition with production and distribution.[44] However, retailing patterns and food availability are crucial determinants of health risk in the RMI where few people produce their own food.

Food retailers in RMI tend to stock a range of foods based on the American diet rather than on a traditional Pacific diet. This includes processed and packaged foods, white flour products, convenience foods and carbonated drinks. Initially these foods were introduced to satisfy the demands of American military personnel resident in RMI, and when the Marshallese acquired a taste for them retailers were happy to supply a larger market. Food aid also contributed to dietary change in RMI. American-oriented nutrition programmes did not recognize the value of local foods such as green coconut milk, and encouraged the consumption of imported foods such as dairy produce and orange juice.[45]

Members of the Marshall Islands Chamber of Commerce have discussed issues of nutrition and poor health. They recognize the linkage between the two and acknowledge their role in the process. The results of their meetings on these issues were twofold. First, they accepted that they were essentially the 'gatekeepers' with regard to the type of food available in urban areas. At the same time they also saw their role as one of providing as broad a range of goods as possible for their customers. They regard it as the customers' responsibility to shop wisely. Second, the most basic element of business is to maintain profitability. In order to do this, at least in the current economic climate, it would be necessary to continue to import relatively cheap goods, even though it is acknowledged that this is almost certainly adding to the incidence of NCDs. Without government subsidies or a marked increase in consumer demand for healthier products, the current situation is likely to remain unchanged. If anything, the anticipated continuing economic recession will mean that consumers will be forced to choose cheaper options when shopping for food, regardless of any adverse health effects.

DISEASE PATTERNS AND LIFESTYLES

Although NCDs have increased markedly, infectious diseases are still significant causes of morbidity and mortality in the Marshall Islands. Health campaigns, including mass immunization and control of epidemics, reduced the incidence of infectious diseases such as tuberculosis, measles, diphtheria, pertussis, tetanus, polio, hepatitis, typhoid and cholera, but most of these diseases still occur from time to time. Antibiotics reduced mortality from respiratory diseases and sepsis, but both are still major causes of death. By 1994 the leading cause of death was cancer, followed by cardiovascular diseases and pneumonia. In 1996 the leading cause of death was cardiovascular disease, followed by sepsis and premature births.[46] It is very likely that some of the sepsis was diabetic sepsis, while lifestyle factors can be presumed to have contributed to cardiovascular disease.

Since high levels of infectious diseases have persisted the Marshall Islands cannot be said to have made a complete health transition. Rather, a dual pattern of infectious and NCDs exists, signifying uneven progress in health. Even when they are not the immediate cause of death, NCDs such as diabetes and hypertension reduce the level of population health and fitness, absorb substantial proportions of the health budget and predispose sufferers to early mortality from other causes.

Differences in disease pattern between urban areas and the outer islands can be found in the Marshall Islands, although the delimiter tends to be the presence or absence of an airstrip rather than a particular location.[47] Because of the high degree of circulation between urban areas and outer islands, those on the periphery prefer to consume urban, store-bought food sent by relatives if they have the opportunity to do so, rather than depending wholly on subsistence. This gives them a health profile similar to those in urban areas, while those who do not have easy access to an airstrip have a lower incidence of NCD, even though they are also likely to have relatively poor health services.

Differences by gender in disease patterns are expected in all countries, and they tend to be particularly marked in peripheral countries where there is uneven progress in health. In the Marshall Islands women are generally more prone to obesity and more than twice as likely to suffer from diabetes than men. However, men appeared to be more likely to suffer complications such as amputations, cardiac problems and cataracts. Women were more likely to die from cancer in 1994 and 1996, and men from most of the other leading causes of death, including accident, sepsis and suicide.[48] Women also suffer from generally poor reproductive health which is directly related to pregnancy, delivery and bearing too many children, with too short birth intervals. Family planning services are available in urban areas and in clinics on outlying atolls. A 1994 survey showed that some 37 per cent of women of reproductive age were currently using contraception, but for the majority this was to stop child bearing after they had already had a large family rather than to delay or space births. There was also some evidence of increasing use of condoms to prevent STDs.[49] At the time of writing there was little or no screening for cervical and breast cancer.

Smoking tobacco is a significant cause of morbidity and mortality in the Marshall Islands. Whereas smoking is generally declining in developed countries, it is still widespread in much of the Pacific, except where religion specifically precludes it. Data for a range of Pacific countries, excluding the Marshall Islands, collected between 1980 and 1994 found prevalence of smoking of between 30 and 90 per cent for men and 1 and 67 per cent for women.[50] There was a general tendency for the prevalence to increase with age, and a slight tendency for prevalence to decline with education, although this was less marked. The pattern is likely to be similar in the

Marshall Islands, where tobacco chewing is common among some of those who do not smoke, including women and school children. Children are able to purchase chewing tobacco, without restriction at local retail outlets, although purchase of cigarettes is restricted to adults. Chewing tobacco is a risk factor for cancers of the mouth and throat and also for tooth decay.

Other lifestyle related causes of death in the Marshall Islands are renal failure and cancer.[51] Both can be associated with a high-sugar, high-fat, low-fibre diet and with alcohol consumption, although they may also have other causes. Non-fatal diseases with a high prevalence in the Marshall Islands include tooth decay, skin diseases, ringworm and scabies. As in some other Pacific countries, gonorrhoea and other sexually transmitted diseases frequently occur in the Marshall Islands. In 1989 almost 4 per cent of urban adults were found to be infected with syphilis, which is fatal in the long term.[52] Contributing factors to the high levels of STDs are increasing promiscuity as a consequence of weakening of tradi-tional social controls, coupled with a reluctance of those at risk to seek treatment for stigmatized conditions. Up until late 1997 only ten cases of HIV/AIDS had been reported in the Marshall Islands, of whom two had died, but the prevalence of this disease will almost certainly increase.[53]

THE NUCLEAR TESTING PROGRAMME

Perhaps the best known cause of ill health in the Marshall Islands, although by no means the leading cause, is the nuclear testing programme conducted by America between 1946 and 1958. This is a highly charged political issue, and the complexity of the relation-ship between radiation and health perceptions is discussed in Chapter 9. The immediate effects of exposure to nuclear testing included flash burns and fatal radiation sickness. Subsequently other conditions have been added to the list of conditions directly attributable to the effects of radiation. At the time of writing suffer-ers of 34 conditions were deemed to be due compensation by the Marshall Islands Nuclear Claims Tribunal, including some cancers, thyroid problems and congenital conditions.[54]

It is not known exactly how many Marshallese were affected by nuclear testing, and the numbers increase continually as new infor-mation becomes available and new diagnoses are made. For example, the Nation-wide Thyroid Study conducted in Majuro in 1994 found that 121 of 1368 people examined had palpable thyroid nodules. Those who had not previously received compensation for thyroid problems received a compensation payment as well as becoming eligible for medical care for this condition under the 177 Health Plan.[55] This plan was initiated by the Marshall Islands government to deal with illnesses presumed to be related to the nuclear test programme.

The impact of radiation on Marshallese health is similar to that of industrial pollution and environmental contamination in some other countries, and can be viewed as a form of environmental contamination resulting from the defence industry. As well as resulting in conditions that are officially recognized as being attributable to nuclear testing, radiation contamination can be a predisposing factor for other disorders. There is currently a lack of hard evidence to prove this, as is also the case with a number of other forms of industrial contamination. New medical facts are continually emerging in relation to exposure to various forms of pollution and contamination, and there is always a chance that further connections could be established. At the time of writing there is controversy over the possible effects of high voltage transmission lines, microwave relays and other forms of power transmission. There is also a continual series of claims seeking to relate various illnesses to exposure to pollutants such as noxious gases, toxic chemicals, food additives and many other forms of contamination. Often it is the least empowered workers who are most at risk of exposure to contamination, and the poorest sectors of the community who have no choice but to live in polluted areas. Among such people, and among the Marshallese, their exposure to contamination is variously a cause of indignation, stress and fatalism as well as illness.

Nuclear testing has been the focus of much attention in the Marshall Islands. However, it is by no means the main reason for the high incidence of diseases such as diabetes, hypertension, cardiovascular problems and cirrhosis. As will be shown in Chapter 9, the Marshallese themselves certainly do not perceive it in this way. Nuclear testing, therefore, should not be emphasized to such an extent that it diverts attention from lifestyle-related causes of ill health, which are more easily preventable.

HEALTH CARE IN THE MARSHALL ISLANDS

Throughout their association the USA has been closely involved in the provision of health care in the Marshall Islands. This has included both investment in national health care and programmes for those directly affected by nuclear testing. In the initial years of Trusteeship health care was generally provided as part of US federal programmes or by the US Navy Department, but aside from treatment of those affected by nuclear testing, which was surrounded in secrecy, health care programmes provided minimal care other than immunization programmes and nutritional advice.

In the early 1960s the Kennedy administration undertook a radical reappraisal of US involvement in the Marshall Islands, and in 1962 there was a threefold increase in funding, of which a substantial proportion was made available for health care. A coordinated health policy was introduced during this period. Strategies such as immunization and the provision of hospital services contributed to declines in infant mortality and increases in life expectancy. At the same time, however, health education was neglected, even though urbanization was increasing, and the Marshallese population was gradually adopting American diets and lifestyle habits which were to contribute to poor health.

Since 1985 health has been administered by the MOHE, which has an annual budget of around US$3 million, derived from Compact funding, federal grants and moneys channelled via US agencies. It is well supplied with advisers from UN agencies such as the WHO and from elsewhere in the region, as well as American advisers from agencies such as the US Center for Disease Control in Atlanta. The MOHE operates two hospitals, in Majuro and Ebeye, and around 70 dispensaries in communities outside the urban centres and in the outer islands. Dispensaries are staffed by health assistants, supported by occasional visits from medexes (paramedics), health educators, and an emergency referral service which utilizes planes and boats to transport patients to the central hospitals. The hospitals provide general and intensive care and have some surgical capability, but serious cases are flown to Hawaii or, more recently, to Manila, which is less costly. The two hospitals also provide outpatient services, dental care and family planning clinics. Although staffed by well-trained medical doctors, the main hospital in Majuro is severely run down and has problems maintaining hygiene. A new hospital has been constructed on

Ebeye to replace a facility which was already very old and seriously run down when visited by one of the authors in 1993. Although construction was already underway at that time, completion was delayed by funding cuts and shortages of materials, and it was still not fully operational at the time of writing.

In the past a distinctive feature of the Marshall Islands' US designed health system was its sharp division into preventive and curative services. Although one positive feature is that this at least ensured that some attention was given to preventive medicine, the rigid separation of function greatly limited the effectiveness of health care. The main problem is that many opportunities to provide preventive health care are lost because it is beyond the capacity or outside the brief of those providing curative services. For example, in the past mothers presenting at a hospital to deliver their seventh or eighth child were not automatically counselled in family planning, even though they might be unlikely to attend a health facility again until they were ready to deliver their next child. Similarly, those presenting with infectious conditions received no counselling on how to prevent them.

In the 1990s the MOHE has placed greater emphasis on primary health care, improved cooperation between preventive and curative services and expanded health and nutrition education and family planning services. Even so, the separation remains, and the capacity to offer good preventive services is limited by low levels of training of dispensary staff, poor record keeping and monitoring, and by the Marshallese orientation towards curative services which has developed over the' years. It must also be observed that long queues and poor service at hospitals and clinics have undoubtedly contributed to loss of faith in modern medicine and a continuing and widespread use of alternative traditional medicine in Marshallese society.

It is interesting to speculate why the USA, like the USSR, did not found a health care system which was more appropriate to the needs of peripheral communities from the outset. Although health care in the Marshall Islands was probably delivered with more compassion and less intimidation than may have been the case in socialist peripheral countries, it does not seem to have been any better in terms of building on traditional systems and involving local communities. Presumably the answer relates to the degree of difficulty of providing comprehensive, integrated health care to prevent illness compared with the relative ease of using the hospital model and emphasizing curative services. In the Marshall Islands, as in the socialist countries, the hospital-based health care model adopted proved too costly for the country to maintain in good condition, even with substantial contributions from the USA. Moreover, its initial lack of attention to primary health care has contributed to a high prevalence of preventable diseases.

COMMON THEMES IN HEALTH AND HEALTH CARE

The Marshallese pattern of health is similar to that of other peripheral groups who have suffered stress and moved away from their traditional lifestyles and traditional diets, such as Native Americans and Australian Aboriginal people.[56] With the exception of illness arising from nuclear testing and other forms of pollution, virtually all other early-onset NCDs in the Marshall Islands are readily preventable. An increase in the consumption of traditional foods with increased dietary fibre, along with a reduction in the consumption of fatty meats, sugar and salt could have an immediate impact on nutrition-related disorders. If this were accompanied by a general increase in physical activity, a reduction in alcohol consumption and the elimination of cigarette smoking, a substantial proportion of the nation's health problems could be eliminated almost overnight. The enormous savings on health care as a result of these changes in lifestyle would probably be sufficient to pay for the provision of safe water, sanitation and garbage disposal to the population as a whole. For these changes to occur, however, would require far reaching socioeconomic change. As is common among marginalized groups throughout the world, many Marshallese appear to have little motivation to take care of their health.

The Marshallese experience has some parallels with the experiences of Uzbekistan and Mongolia. When the Soviet Empire disintegrated those who were unable to take advantage of the entrepreneurial opportunities offered by the shift to a market economy became increasingly disadvantaged by the new globalization. Their incomes dwindled relative to those of the successful entrepreneurs, while both access to and the quality of health services deteriorated. In the 1990s these disadvantaged groups were manifesting symptoms of unhealthy lifestyles similar to those displayed by the Marshallese. In all three countries substantial proportions of the population consume poor diets, and/or indulge in heavy smoking and drinking.

Mongolia and Uzbekistan also exhibit regional differences in disease patterns, as are found in the Marshall Islands. For example, in Uzbekistan diseases of the alimentary tract and infectious diseases are more common among the rural population, while cardiovascular diseases and malignant tumours are more often found among the urban population.[57] In the Aral Sea region, which has been subject to both socioeconomic disruption and environmental crisis, the main illnesses are anaemia, cardiovascular and kidney disease, and sickness rates are estimated to be from 50 to 70 per cent higher than the national average.

Obesity does not yet appear to be a significant concern of health authorities in either Mongolia or Uzbekistan, and there is certainly little obesity to be observed on the streets of Ulaanbaatar and Tashkent. The diets generally consumed by the poor in these countries tend to be lower in calories than typical Pacific diets, where the cheapest imported food items tend to be manufactured products which are high in fat, sugar and salt. Another contributing factor is that more people are engaged in active occupations such as agriculture, and there is less unemployment in urban areas. There are also more opportunities for recreational physical activity in both Mongolia and Uzbekistan compared with the Marshall Islands. It is also possible that the different physical attributes of Marshallese, who are generally short in stature with a genetic propensity to store fat efficiently, make them more prone to obesity than Mongolians and Uzbeks.

An increase in obesity in Mongolia and Uzbekistan could occur as economic conditions improve, more people become involved in the market economy and more people adopt high calorie diets and sedentary lifestyles. For example, the MirBurger fast food chain is already selling American-style hamburgers and fried potato chips in Tashkent. Although relatively expensive compared with other options, MirBurger attracts a large clientele of fashion-conscious young people. It could signify the beginning of a swing towards Western 'junk food' which has a greater potential to cause obesity.

The most striking thing about the Marshallese case is that, compared with Mongolia and Uzbekistan, there appear to be fewer obstacles to the achievement of good health. Given the small population size, the substantial levels of economic assistance, the relatively good living environment, and the obvious improvements that could be made, it seems surprising that the Marshallese do not have generally good health. This view is shared by government and health officials in the Marshall Islands, who have made health education programmes and primary health care a key focus of the national health strategy. Yet even though most Marshallese have been exposed to health education programmes and have been made well aware of how and why they should change their lifestyles, many have not modified their behaviour. Among the Marshallese, as among many other marginalized groups, high-risk health behaviour persists even when it could be avoided.

In order to further explore the reasons why many Marshallese have adopted unhealthy lifestyles, the following chapters investigate more closely the factors which have shaped Marshallese perceptions and attitudes. Chapter 8 considers social and cultural patterns, and day-to-day life in the Marshall Islands. Chapter 9 looks at the way Marshallese perceive health and the factors which they believe to be the external and sociological determinants of their health. These chapters show that the reality is often different from the popular image of factors affecting health behaviour, and demonstrate that it is necessary to fully understand health perceptions and responses to socioeconomic forces in order to formulate appropriate health strategies.

Chapter 8

A Portrait of Life at the Periphery

This chapter looks at the way in which life in the Marshall Islands has been shaped by remoteness, economic marginalization and its dependent relationship with the USA and by the unique characteristics of Marshallese culture and society, which have shaped Marshallese responses to these external factors.

These factors have combined to determine the lifestyle options and choices which affect health. Although other countries are affected by different sets of factors, common themes can be identified. For example, Russian domination of Mongolia and Uzbekistan defined their locations as peripheral, and reduced their capacity for self-sufficiency, despite both having substantial populations and a generous endowment of land and raw materials to support industrialization. Even though the Marshall Islands has a very small population and a minute land area deficient in soils and mineral resources, it is rich in marine resources. As in Mongolia and Uzbekistan, the relationship with a superpower, in this case the USA, has prevented the Marshall Islands from developing self-sufficiency based on greater utilization of marine resources.

THE PHYSICAL ENVIRONMENT

One of the most important factors shaping life in the Marshall Islands is physical isolation. The Marshall Islands represents an extreme example of a remote geographical location, which impacts strongly on day-to-day living. Not only is the country as a whole very remote from the USA, its country of reference, but its own physical structure, a scattering of tiny atolls across a vast area of the Pacific Ocean, isolates groups within the country. Geographical remoteness also contributes to social as well as to economic isolation, and to the preservation of a strong traditional culture, even though there has been considerable infiltration of American values.

Coral atolls provide a unique living experience. In the Marshall Islands, the highest point, on Wotje Atoll, is only 10 metres above sea level, and most is no more than 2 metres above sea level. The larger atolls comprise long, sinuous strips of land, most only 100–200 metres or so in width, fading into dotted lines of islands at their extremities. Smaller atolls may be no more than a string of tiny islands. Many of the lagoons are vast, with the lands at the far side hidden below the horizon. Kwajalein, the world's largest coral atoll, is more than 100 kilometres from one end to the other. Some of the atolls have only a few hectares of dry land, and even the largest has no more than 10 square kilometres.

Majuro is only 7 degrees north of the Equator, and has a hot and wet equatorial climate. The climate is drier in the northern atolls including Bikini, Enewatak and Rongelap. All of the Marshall Islands have a marked dry and wet season. The wettest months are October and November and the driest are December to April, but there is little variation in the mean temperature, which hovers around 27 degrees Celsius. The wetter islands to the south support lush growth when rainfall is good, and are thickly wooded. Even so, agricultural production is constrained by salination and thin coral soils. Atoll soils are marginal, and not really soil in the conventional sense since they are mostly sand and silt-sized pieces of limestone rather than soil, silt and clay. They are typically low in organic carbon, nitrogen and potassium. Iron, manganese and zinc are deficient or unavailable to plants because of high phosphate levels caused by the limestone. Ground water is usually saline, the activity of soil micro-organisms is limited, and soil has low water holding capacity because of its coarse texture, which is due to the predominance of physical rather than chemical weathering.[1]

Food plants with a high salt tolerance, which grow well in the Marshall Islands, include arrowroot, asparagus, beet, coconut, kale, pandanus, papaya and spinach. Breadfruit has low salt tolerance but is well adapted to atoll soils, as are cabbage and cantaloupe.[2] Bananas and, more recently, pumpkin, are also grown successfully. Some varieties of taro will grow in the Marshall Islands, but require intensive care and the digging of pits. By the late 1960s islanders on at least one atoll said they were reluctant to grow taro because of the effort required.[3] Other foods like pandanus, arrowroot and breadfruit were also generally subject to complex processing and preparation before eating, but perhaps because food preparation is women's work while digging is men's work, this apparently proved less of a deterrent. Fish are still abundant throughout the Marshall Islands and an important food source, especially in the outer islands.

Because of the heat and humidity, most people shelter in houses or under palm trees during the main part of the day or, in urban areas, in air-conditioned buildings. In the wet season rainfall is often torrential, and the roads on the main islands are quickly flooded. In Majuro the side streets are often flooded, and large potholes have been scoured out by repeated flooding and the constant traffic of taxis and private vehicles. Even though the sea is close by, drainage is poor and large pools of water remain on the roads for several days after rain has stopped. The combination of enervating heat and frequent heavy rain restricts movement. The majority of urban Marshallese cannot afford a car and rely on taxis, unless they have access to a government vehicle. It can be difficult to find a seat in a taxi on a wet day, and it is common for people to break appointments or to fail to turn up for work when it rains.

Food quickly spoils in the moist hot climate unless it is refrigerated, and buildings deteriorate rapidly unless regularly maintained. Salt spray, frequent immersion in brackish puddles and scraping on uneven road surfaces dramatically shortens the life of motor vehicles. Regular showers in fresh water would seem to be an essential requirement for everyday health and comfort, but are often unavailable to both rural and urban Marshallese because of water shortages during dry periods. Washing in the lagoon leaves the body and hair caked with salt, and may itself present a health hazard because of pollution near urban areas.

SOCIAL STRUCTURE

Although external influences and the adoption of a more 'Westernized' lifestyle have led to some adaptations, traditional Marshallese culture remains strong. Marshallese social structure is rigid and hierarchical, with clearly defined roles for each strata of society. At the top of the social hierarchy are the 'iroij' (hereditary chiefs). The iroij have ultimate control over land tenure, resource use and distribution and dispute settlement. Traditionally, the iroij has a duty of care to his people, and they must obey him. They must accept his distribution of land and goods and not question his decisions. They are obliged to wait for his decisions, and he, in turn, is obliged to make decisions on their behalf. The iroij is autocratic, however, and subjects fear that if they complain about his decisions they will lose what assets they already have. The 'alap' (clan heads) maintain lands and supervise daily activities, and the 'rijerbal' (workers) are responsible for the daily work of subsistence, construction and agriculture.[4] The core of Marshallese culture is respect for leaders and for the older generation. An informant commented that a wife who answers back to her husband will be beaten, and it is unthinkable to question the judgement of elders.

Land inheritance in traditional Marshallese society is matrilineal. This ensured respect for women, although most of the decisions relating to its distribution were determined by custom or were made by the woman's male kin. Complex rules govern the distribution of land, which is generally classified into 12 categories, ranging from land which belongs to a whole lineage (iman bwij) to land given by a husband as a gift to his wife (kitdre).[5] Although land ownership was, and still is, an important determinant of societal roles, the land tenure system is one aspect of traditional Marshallese culture that has been eroded by contact with capitalism. Land trading is now possible, and some have profited substantially from land sales, while others have sold their primary asset for little return.[6] One informant reported that he had been able to buy land at bargain prices because of the eagerness of some individuals to acquire status symbols such as motor vehicles.

Although the traditional social order remains a central part of contemporary Marshallese life, it has been overlaid with a political administrative model based on ideals introduced during the period of Trusteeship. The Republic is headed by the President and there is an elected Parliament. In some respects the function of government resembles Western liberal democratic systems, but parallel to this the older system of respect and patronage continues to function, and traditional leaders figure prominently in government. This has inhibited the formation of a significant parliamentary opposition party, which would run directly counter to traditional practices. An illustration of how modern democratic principles are blended with traditional custom was the process of selecting a successor when President Amata Kabua died in 1996. His kinsman, Imata Kabua, was one of the few eligible people who could succeed him in the short term, because, according to custom, an unrelated person would not have been permitted to live in the late President's house, while the construction of a new Presidential House would have been costly and time consuming.

Throughout the succession of German, Japanese and American colonial regimes, the Marshallese have protected their national identity by retaining the essential elements of their culture. Other than during the Japanese rule there has been little settlement by outsiders, and even then the Japanese administrators did not encourage integration with the islanders. The main external influences on Marshallese society have been the imbalances of wealth and power created by the political control of incoming Trusteeship funds, the Compact and some land rental agreements, rather than from the introduction of new forms of government.

In traditional Marshallese society, as in most traditional societies, there was a disparity of wealth between the ruling and lower classes. Modernization in the Marshall Islands has reinforced this pattern. The emergence of higher income groups does not automatically lead to social tension or conflict. A situation of marked income disparities need not be problematic if the basic needs of all members of the community are met. Problems arise only when growing numbers of the people are faced with poor living conditions, deteriorating service provision and raised expectations of the perceived benefits of a progressively more consumerist lifestyle.

Traditional social structures tend to be relatively successful in providing a safety net for those not fully participating in the introduced political and economic system. In the Marshall Islands this mechanism is still functioning. For example, an informant employed in the public sector reported that he was paying for the education of several children of unemployed relatives. However, the unusual pressures of the transition towards the lifestyle of Western societies, and the uneven distribution of the benefits of modernization throughout Marshallese society, is subjecting this traditional support system to growing strain.

This conjunction of traditional and modern social mechanisms has parallels in other marginalized groups and emerging societies, but it is more common to find that groups of people within a single society retain traditional cultural practices to varying extents. For example, in Uzbekistan the practice of the traditional Islamic religion, which was driven underground during the Soviet era, is rapidly strengthening among the poorest groups of society. In contrast, those who have benefited most from modernization and the modern economy have tended not to adopt the more conservative aspects of Muslim culture, but continue to live in nuclear families and to dress in modern Western clothing.

SOCIALIZATION AND EDUCATION

The way in which Marshallese children are socialized is fundamental to the perpetuation of a strong Marshallese culture. The norm in Marshallese society is for children to have more contact with older children and with grandparents than with their parents. This is facilitated by the common practice of living in extended family households consisting of a dozen or more related people. In such households the parents of young children and adolescents are likely to be the main breadwinners in the household, and so are most often busy or absent. As a consequence children receive most of their socialization from siblings or grandparents, and only infrequently experience intensive and mentally stimulating interaction with their mother or father. It must be noted, however, that it is becoming more common for Marshallese with higher status occupations and higher incomes to live in nuclear households, where children have more interaction with their parents, even though they retain strong ties with family members living outside their household.

Older siblings normally spend long hours caring for their younger brothers and sisters by carrying them about or letting them follow along, sometimes restraining them when they risk wandering into danger. Older siblings are not generally permitted to physically punish younger siblings. If physical violence is used parents may intervene with threats and may punish the sibling carer. This leads to the development of 'sibling solidarity', causing siblings to stick together. 'Indeed, adult siblings may disagree; they may avoid one another, but they do not fight'.[7] Another feature of Marshallese sibling carers is that they seldom use praise and positive reinforcement to socialize younger children,[8] and this persists into interactions in adulthood. When complemented on the quality of his work, one of our field assistants explained that in Marshallese culture it is inappropriate to give lavish praise to anyone in the presence of others, since this singles them out as an individual and causes embarrassment.

Young children thus may live much of their life in a fairly public community, which encourages them to develop strong community bonds and to avoid drawing attention to themselves in ways which might attract attention, arouse jealousy or anger or anything else that might weaken the sibling bond. A school counsellor said that children learn their place in society by observing other children; parents and other adults do not tell them what to do. In particular, children learn to be quiet in the company of adults and not to venture opinions or to draw attention to themselves. Even though grandparents are more likely to tell stories and interact with grandchildren in a loving way, from a very early age parents teach children to be very respectful to their grandparents and never to contradict or answer them back. This, too, encourages passive rather than active interactions.

One respondent remarked that Marshallese do not like their children to go to a nursery or be cared for by someone outside their family because a stranger might tell them something their parents would not want them to hear. It is likely that the problem might not be so much what the children are told, as concern about the type of personality they might develop. For example, it would be regarded as socially disruptive if a pre-school teacher encouraged children to speak out for themselves and ask questions, and praised them for doing so

In the urban areas unsupervised bands of children of all ages play around settlements and in the streets. Sometimes toddlers can be found straying alone on public roads with no one in sight who might be in any way responsible for them, perhaps as far as 50 or 100 metres from the nearest building. Usually they appeared cheerful and unconcerned, and indeed, it is rare to hear a child crying in the Marshall Islands. Away from adult company children up to age seven or eight appear to be confident and outgoing. They are friendly and sometimes a little cheeky to passing foreigners, and many do not hesitate to speak to or take the hand of a stranger and accompany them to the limits of their territory. Informants suggested that by age seven children generally stop answering back to their parents, and we found that children from about school age onward appear to be less outgoing towards strangers. This could, of course, be related to their experiences with teachers and a new expectation that adult strangers were likely to ask them difficult questions. A favourite activity of adolescent boys is to establish gangs with their own rituals and signs, which contribute to the close bonding of sibling groups.

Even though they tend not to interact with their children in the intensive, one-on-one fashion usual in Western nuclear families, Marshallese parents love and value their children enormously, and lavish as much expenditure on them as they can afford. When circumstances permit, children are well dressed and provided with expensive toys and educational needs. Paradoxically, an important cause of poor nutrition among Marshallese children is parents feeding them on carbonated drinks, biscuits and sweets rather than nutritious foods, because these sweet 'junk food' items are costly and therefore assumed to be good. Parents who feed their children Cheeseballs for breakfast are not deliberately neglecting them but genuinely believe they are doing the best they can for them.[9]

The Marshall Islands has a dual system of private and public education up to secondary school level. Most of the private schools, which charge fees, are run by church groups. In 1994–1995 there were 103 elementary schools in the Marshall Islands, of which 27 were private.[10] Ten of the private schools were in Majuro. There were 13 secondary schools, of which only one in Majuro and one in Jaluit were public. There were six private high schools in Majuro, three on Kwajeliein, and one each in Ailinglaplap and Namu.[11] By far the largest high school was the Marshall Islands High School, the public High School in Rita on Majuro, which had more than 700 pupils.

From a statistical perspective the Marshallese population is highly literate; some 90 per cent were classified as literate in 1988.[12] However, many have only minimal skills in either Marshallese or English, which would tend to discourage them from reading and writing. For many, most of their reading would be done in church. Literacy and language is an area of contention in the school syllabus. Under the American system Marshallese children were taught to read and write in English first, and then learned Marshallese later on. In the 1990s there was growing concern that many children were leaving primary school still unable to write in Marshallese, and a fear that this would weaken the Marshallese cultural heritage. This led to a reversal of the policy, and children are now taught to read and write first in Marshallese, with English writing introduced only in third grade. It is too early to gauge the effect of this policy. Although it is easy to sympathize with the nationalist objectives, it does pose the very real risk that children will not acquire good reading and writing skills in English, which is the language of government and commerce. In the relatively passive learning environment of Marshallese elementary schools, many children have acquired only limited English skills, even when it was taught as the first language.

One of the problems of education in the Marshall Islands is that many elementary school teachers themselves have only limited education and limited teaching skills. Under the American system and up until 1997, many of the outer island elementary schools were supported by American Peace Corps educators, but they too were often inexperienced. Because children tend to be shy and non-participatory, in both elementary and high schools teachers tend to rely on writing notes up on the board and rote learning rather than on stimulating student initiative. Overall, elementary education is generally weak, and many children emerge poorly prepared for high school. Marshallese opinions differ as to which schools are the best, but generally informants seemed to think that private schools give a better education. Several informants sent their children to a school run by a religious denomination other than their own because they believed that it provided a better education. The most affluent Marshallese prefer to send their children 'off island' for secondary education in Hawaii, Fiji or even further afield.

Teachers at the Marshall Islands High School told how the abolition of the school lunch programme, a 1995 economy measure, has increased the difficulty of teaching by enhancing social class differences between children. Children from wealthier homes can afford to bring attractive lunches or to purchase their lunch at the nearby shops, but children from poorer homes may have little or no lunch or else may need to go home for lunch. This not only excludes them from the society of others at school, but can also make them late for afternoon classes. Most disadvantaged of all and most likely to drop out of school are children from the outer islands who are staying with 'guardian' relatives living near the high school. These children tend to find city life unfamiliar and to have less money than their peers, but may have no one to turn to with their problems.[13] Shyness may cause them to perform less well at school compared with their guardian's own children, and they are often the first called upon to help in the home or to care for younger children. This, in turn, may lead to a poor school performance. A 1985 study of runaway Marshallese girls, most of whom had fallen into prostitution, found they had usually dropped out of school because they were performing poorly. These girls also said they were unable to tolerate the requirement that they should be quiet and self-effacing and wait at home for a suitor.[14]

LIFE IN MAJURO AND EBEYE

An American woman who went to Majuro in the 1960s to marry her Marshallese fiancé told us that he had warned her not to expect a 'Pacific Paradise'. She said he had prepared her well for the remoteness and the simple, austere life she found in Majuro at that time. Although some islands still reflect the stereotype imagery of the beautiful, unspoiled, island paradise, the main settlements of Majuro are congested and shabby, and Ebeye resembles a densely packed squatter settlement such as one might expect to find in poorer parts of South-East Asia.

Although life can be very comfortable in the quality housing and luxurious green landscapes of Long Island and Ajeltake, the inner Majuro suburbs of Rita, Darrit-Uliga-Delap (DUD), are densely settled with little space between houses, which are uncoordinated and under-serviced. Families of 12 or more may live in a typical poorly ventilated, two-room concrete block structure sometimes as small as 5 metres square and with an unlined iron roof, or in a decaying mobile home. Windows are commonly unglazed and washing and cooking facilities are often rudimentary. Most houses have toilet facilities and piped water inside or nearby, but drainage and sanitation is poor. Fifty per cent of the population of the Marshall Islands were estimated to lack access to safe water in 1994.[15] In 1988 some 11,200 persons lived in an area of less than 1.5 square kilometres in the DUD area of Majuro and more than 8000 people lived on Ebeye's 0.36 square kilometres.[16] This is approximately the same density as in London or Munich.

There is a designated garbage dump in Majuro and scheduled garbage collections, but the lagoon and ocean are widely used for refuse disposal. Although most people keep their house surrounds tidy, picking up garbage and sweeping leaves, garbage litters the roadsides and lagoon shores. Perhaps this is regarded as neutral ground for which no one is designated as having responsibility. Pedestrians walking along poorly lit streets at night risk injury from stumbling on discarded rubbish and items such as dislodged sheets of roofing iron.

Inspection of the garbage littering the shores reveals that it is mainly aluminium cans, bottles and paper, plastics and polystyrenes, which are mostly packaging. These recyclable items are bulked out with biodegradable refuse, such as coconut husks and food remains, which could degrade quickly if they were the only form of litter. A big litter problem is disposable nappies. Most urban Marshallese mothers have adopted the American habit of using disposable rather than reusable nappies for their children. Although this is clearly easier than washing nappies where household facilities are limited, they are an expensive choice, costing between US$0.3 and 0.7 each, depending on size. This not only strains slender household budgets but also adds considerably to waste disposal problems, and many end up in the lagoon, where they have even been known to clog speedboat motors.

Majuro houses commonly have vivid green, pink or blue exteriors faded into dinginess or disfigured with graffiti which demarcate the territories of youth gangs. Although houses are often shaded with coconut or breadfruit trees, they tend to be very hot during the day unless air-conditioned. Higher quality housing may be large with a garden, but few have vegetable gardens. Flower-decked, thick concrete gravestones, of both adult and child length, mark burial sites beside many of the homes of the living. On Ebeye space is at a premium, with wall-to-wall houses and very few trees. A ring road and a few cross-links separate the coastal and inner blocks of houses. Surprisingly, it is often packed with cruising cars in the evenings, even though one could reach any part of the island on foot in 15 minutes or less. By the 1980s there were more than 200 motor vehicles on Ebeye, even though there were only 3 kilometres of road.[17]

Even by 1964 Ebeye was crowded and described by a former Trust Territory representative as a 'stunning social revolution ... it's astonishing how quickly the Marshallese have learned to want such 20th century appliances as electric refrigerators, automatic toasters and tape recorders. And they want them right now'.[18] Large retail stores in Majuro and Ebeye are reasonably well stocked with imported foods and consumer goods, and there are many family mini-stores which supply immediate household needs. As discussed in Chapter 7, the retailing emphasis on imported rather than local foods makes a significant contribution to unhealthy lifestyles in RMI.

In 1988 the average household size in the Marshall Islands was 8.6. For Majuro as whole it was 8.8 and for Kwajalein it was 9.8,[19] but it is not uncommon for households in Majuro and Ebeye to comprise as many as 30 residents.[20] With limited land areas and low agricultural productivity, Majuro dwellers have ceased to rely on traditional crops and now purchase virtually all their needs from local mini-markets or larger retail stores. This has made them extremely vulnerable to changing economic conditions. Employment in the public sector forms the largest and most lucrative percentage of the wage economy. The implementation of cut backs as part of structural adjustment since 1995 has not only reduced job opportunities in a context where a significant proportion of the labour force is unemployed, but also seriously eroded household security. In typical Marshallese extended families, one or two weekly pay cheques could be supporting many people. Similarly, the salary from employment at the United States Army at Kwajalein Atoll (USAKA) base may to be used to support many family members on Ebeye.

Despite what often appear to be poor living conditions in the urban areas, especially on Ebeye, there seems to be no reversal in the trend of urban drift. These two centres continue to attract both short-stayers and settlers from the outer islands. Some of the outer islanders live temporarily with relatives in the centres, occasionally for work and often while attending high school or the College of the Marshall Islands in Majuro. Those with regular employment are more fixed. Others with a less secure footing in the main centres shuttle back and forth, sometimes staying with relatives in the main centres and at other times returning to more traditional lifestyles. This relieves some pressure on the congested and overcrowded main centres, but also spreads urban influences to the outer islands. Several respondents noted that it was common for those returning to the outer islands to take foodstuffs and other goods normally only available in Majuro or Ebeye.

Non-Marshallese might consider life in crowded and unsanitary conditions to be less appealing than alternatives in the outer islands. Yet clearly there remains a desire among Marshallese to migrate towards these centres. One respondent told us that life was even more desirable on Ebeye than Majuro. Although it was acknowledged that the physical environment is inferior, this was seen as being outweighed by other factors. Interestingly, he said there was a greater sense of 'village life' and stronger traditions on Ebeye. It is also well known that average per capita incomes on Ebeye are up to five times those elsewhere in the country, as a consequence of the annual rental of approximately US$10 million paid by USAKA to local landowners. The fact that many Ebeye residents receive only a small share of these high incomes does not seem to reduce the appeal of Ebeye.

TRANSPORT AND COMMUNICATIONS

The extent of the Marshall Islands territory over some 30 remote and dispersed coral atolls makes travelling and moving things from one part of the country to another expensive, time consuming, inconvenient, irregular and unreliable. Since very little food and few commodities are produced locally, virtually everything is imported, so freight movements are an essential to support the community, and transport costs are a significant component in national expenditure.

Road transport is generally limited because of the smallness of most islands. In 1995 the Marshall Islands had a total of 1665 registered motor vehicles, of which 1305 were sedan cars and pickup trucks.[21] Only Kwajalein and Majuro have significant road networks. USAKA has its own network of roads to service the base while the ring road on Ebeye is a short service road. Road transport is very important on Majuro, which has a 48 kilometre strip as a consequence of some causeway building and a two-lane arched bridge which connects Long Island to Majuro. This 48 km stretch of road includes a very heavily used section between Rita and the airport, and a less heavily used section from the airport to Laura. It allows Laura and Ajeltake residents to commute to Majuro for work or education if they wish, and has led some high income families to construct quality housing in the very pleasant surroundings of Long Island and south of the airport. Even so, this main road is often poorly maintained because it erodes very quickly under the pressure of traffic and heavy rains.

Despite low speed limits of 40 km per hour in built up areas and 70 km per hour south of the airport, it is hazardous to drive, especially between the airport and Rita, because of semi-concealed speed humps and very large pot holes which are often hidden under large ponds of water. Another hazard is inexperienced drivers who may drift across the road. At the time of writing Japanese funds had been made available for resurfacing and upgrading of the main road.

Container ships from America and Asia regularly stop at Majuro and Kwajalein, and many small vessels ply between the atolls, but distances are long. Although distance does not necessarily add proportionally to the cost of shipping, it increases the difficulty of handling perishables, such as fish and frozen goods. It also makes it costly to export low value goods, such as materials that could be recycled. This helps to explain the large quantities of decaying machinery and other refuse that litter the shores in most settled areas.

The Marshall Islands is an out-of-the-way place for most travellers, and costly to reach by air. It is considerably more expensive to purchase a return air ticket to the Marshall Islands from Australia or from the UK than to purchase a round the world ticket from either country. Even from the West Coast of the USA it is an expensive trip, via Honolulu. The national airline, Air Marshalls, flies between Fiji and the Marshall Islands six times a week via Kiribati and Tuvalu, this route has been plagued by service difficulties due to mechanical failures. The 1996 purchase of a US$16 million SAAB turbo-prop aircraft has done little to improve the situation and the new aircraft is frequently unable to take off on schedule because servicing is needed.

Travel within the Marshall Islands is limited and expensive. Air Marshalls had only three planes at the time of writing and was servicing around 30 widely dispersed internal locations and the Fiji route with no backup aircraft. Many flights between atolls are also delayed by mechanical breakdowns and bad weather, and there is a high risk of passengers being stranded. No part of the country is accessible by air seven days a week. Continental Micronesia, a US airline, runs a service between Honolulu and Guam several times a week, which touches down at both Majuro and Kwajalein, thus providing both an internal and an international service. However, Marshallese are critical of Continental's dealings with the Marshall Islands. In particular they blame Continental for competition which caused Air Marshalls to make a heavy loss on, and eventually to abandon, flights between Majuro and Honolulu.

Mail services between the Marshall Islands and the rest of the world are slow and unreliable. In late 1997 there were only one or two mail deliveries to the Marshall Islands in a period of several months. In the main centres the domestic telephone system is often congested, and a scarcity of inward lines in government departments makes contacting people by phone tedious and time consuming. Only Majuro and Ebeye have landline telephone systems. Communication between atolls is by radio telephone. International telephone calls are very expensive, and this high cost passes on to fax and electronic mail. A respondent working in an international NGO observed that in any event there is a tendency for people not to act on faxes and phone calls received from abroad until the sender actually appears in the Marshall Islands.

SPORT, ENTERTAINMENT AND RECREATION

To the casual observer there appear to be few sources of entertainment, especially for young people. Outdoors, as in most countries, children play around the houses and in the street. School age children and adolescents play volleyball and basketball wherever they can find a space, but in Majuro and Ebeye there are few spaces large enough to support games such as baseball, soccer or even an athletics track, and generally provision is not made for such sports. A basketball court outside the College of the Marshall Islands in Majuro is floodlit and used for an organized multi-level basketball league competition, which attracts a large and enthusiastic crowd of onlookers. Most other facilities for volleyball and basketball are inferior, with players forced to use uneven surfaces and limited spaces. There is also a bowling alley which runs league competitions, and two tennis courts.

Children and young men predominate on the basketball and volleyball courts; adolescent girls and older men are seen less often, and women hardly ever. The newly built gymnasium in Majuro offers a large indoor covered space, but has been set up primarily as an auditorium and sports hall with basketball courts and volleyball nets; it lacks the exercise machines commonly found in such facilities. There is a small, private gym nearby which also runs classes in martial arts. Walking was cited by numerous respondents as an increasingly popular health-related activity, and part of the Diabetes Reversal Program discussed elsewhere in this book. Even so, it is generally only comfortable to walk in the early mornings and evenings, and the only place to walk is along the uneven, litter strewn and often inundated roads. Joggers are a rare sight.

More affluent households in the urban areas are well equipped with TV, video and sound equipment, and there are numerous video hire shops. In these households children watch TV and play computer games such as Nintendo®. Japanese and British TV channels and several major American TV networks are available by satellite. This gives exposure to the heavy advertising of American consumer products on American Network TV. There is no local censorship, although a respondent said that at one time there was a proposal to restrict foreign transmissions to cartoons for children. At the time of writing a wide variety of programmes were broadcast, including those depicting sexual intimacy and near-nudity, which many Marshallese see as unacceptable behaviour for their own people. A respondent commented that programmes such as aerobics workouts featuring scantily clad instructors, which are broadcast each day, are more often interpreted as soft pornography than as a pathway to the attainment of physical fitness, and would certainly be switched off by the older generation.

Movies have public showings in the urban centres, and a local TV station in Majuro broadcasts mostly advertisements and personal greeting messages. At the time of writing the Australian and New Zealand governments were funding a project to produce a series of TV programmes on local history, arts and culture but these programmes were broadcast for only one hour per week. Although most households own a transistor radio/tape player and Walkman® tape players are common, many of the poorer urban households do not own a TV or video player. There are local radio stations in Ebeye and Majuro broadcasting in Marshallese and playing local as well as international music. Sometimes they operate with only a skeleton staff and a single CD may be repeated over and over for many hours. Many more Marshallese tune into the live radio broadcasts of parliamentary debates as the scale and intimacy of Marshallese culture and society encourage the electorate to take an interest in parliamentary business. Not only will events there be likely to have a direct impact on the lives of most listeners, it is also quite likely that they will know, or even be related to, many politicians.

Beer is readily available at main retail outlets and at local mini-shops, and spirits are cheap at some of the major retailing outlets in the urban areas. Residents are required to obtain a drinking permit, which serves to restrict underage drinking and can be withdrawn as a punitive measure if drinkers misbehave. Policing of drinking, however, is limited and erratic. There is some policing of drink-driving, but it is not unusual to see severely intoxicated people drive themselves home after late night functions. Bars in the main hotels and clubs on Majuro and Ebeye attract a regular clientele of both foreign and local drinkers, and there are also many local drinking spots. Bingo and card games are popular, and bets are placed on the outcomes. There are also several pool halls, largely patronized by adolescent boys. There are regular discos at weekends, some patronized by adolescents and some by slightly older groups. The discos are dark, crowded and encourage heavy drinking and smoking. Few of these activities are available in the outer islands. Several atolls, including Arno which is very close to Majuro, have banned alcohol.

Marshallese place a high value on social events such as birthday parties, especially infants' first birthday parties, funerals and wedding celebrations, which require extensive and expensive hospitality. Customary obligation ceremonies, which formerly would have been met with home produced foods, now demand lavish catering with imported foods, rental of facilities, disposable plates and plastic cutlery, and distribution of gifts. Families may raise bank loans to meet such obligations and may spend as much as US$10,000 for a first birthday party or a funeral.[22] In addition, Marshallese seem to welcome any other excuse to hold a party or a parade. Christmas is a season of much partying and street parades, and large crowds turn out to participate. The main government departments hold office parties with lavish feasts of fish, pork, rice, special dishes such as pumpkin in coconut and salads, and copious amounts of alcohol. Over-catering at social events is never a problem for Marshallese. Leftover food is served out on to paper plates which are covered with tin foil and distributed to guests to take home.

RELIGION

Organized religion is a central part of Marshallese life. It provides moral guidance, cultural reinforcement, social life and entertainment. The overwhelming majority of Marshallese are practising Christians, who attend church every Sunday and often several times during the week as well. Church services in the Marshall Islands include enthusiastic community singing, which is a subject of great pride among congregations. Despite the small total population size, there is considerable religious diversity. The main churches are The United Church of Christ, Assembly of God, Catholic, Reformed Congregational, Mormon (Church of the Latter Day

Saints), Bukot Non Jesus, and Seventh Day Adventist. There are also smaller percentages of Baptist, Jehovah's Witnesses, Salvation Army, Baha'i and other groups, mainly introduced by missions from America or other developed countries. Some members of ethnic minority groups such as the Japanese and Koreans may also practise non-Christian religions.

Participation in a church group reinforces the Marshallese sense of community which might otherwise be eroded by the pressures of urbanization and economic hardship, bringing together both young and old. At the same time the strong moral code of the church also helps to maintain social order. The requirement that Christians accept without question the teachings of God is consistent with the hierarchical nature of Marshallese traditional culture. It fosters acceptance and faith in leadership. Christian churches also tend to emphasize that life is hard, and suffering on Earth will be rewarded in the hereafter. This is consistent with the Marshallese experience of nuclear testing, and may foster a tendency to be philosophical about day-to-day problems and to look forward to their resolution after death. This will be discussed further in Chapter 9.

Several informants criticized the establishment of breakaway churches in the Marshall Islands following rifts within congregations. One such example is Bukot Non Jesus, which was formed after a disagreement among supporters of The United Church of Christ. It was also observed by informants on several occasions that not all church-goers observe the ten commandments, and some simply pay lip-service to religion by attending church. This is, of course, a universal problem, which may appear to be exaggerated in the Marshall Islands because such a large percentage of the population does attend church. Elsewhere, where the societal importance of church attendance is less emphasized, it is more likely that people who do not intend to observe the ten commandments do not appear in churches.

LIFE IN THE OUTER ISLANDS

Although life on the outer islands presents a striking contrast to life in the urban areas in terms of the built environment, in fact it may not be very different at all in terms of social organization. Outer islands are regarded as stronger centres of traditional values, but this may be more an indication of their older age structure than of a different set of values. Similarly, if the people on the outer islands cultivate more traditional foods and live more active lives it is from necessity not design. As discussed elsewhere, an informant from an NGO concerned with the Diabetes Reversal Program spoke of a direct association between proximity to an airstrip and the consumption of an unhealthy western diet. Others spoke of sending imported food and goods to relatives in the outer islands because they were valued items and so the outer island residents should be able to enjoy them. The main income earning activities for outer islands residents are copra and handicrafts. Lack of refrigeration limits opportunities for commercial fishing.

Lack of services or cheap regular transport leave outer islanders little alternative but to follow traditional lifestyles and pursue traditional pastimes. Although many have transistor radios, modern entertainment is otherwise limited by the need to rely on petrol generators for electricity. Even the tourist operation on Mili Atoll has to turn guests away at times because it does not have a generator available. None the less, high levels of mobility, especially movement to urban areas for education and employment, have smoothed out significant differences in outlook between urban and rural Marshallese. Although around 30 per cent of the population reside outside the main urban areas, data are lacking on what proportion have never lived anywhere else. Since in many ways the outer islands are perceived by urban Marshallese as dormitory suburbs rather than as independent economic entities, it is likely that many residents on outer islands have spent time living in urban areas. One island which does not seem to fit this model is Jaluit, which is widely regarded as being more self-contained, and as having a more independent and progressive outlook. Informants from Jaluit suggested that the Jaluit people are more likely to stick together and stay on their own island.

Virtually all outer island residents have close ties with urban residents, and use these contacts to facilitate visits to urban centres and the exchange of goods, as well as to accommodate children who need to attend high school. Urban Marshallese with higher incomes may visit relatives in the outer islands for holidays, to relax, to fish in the lagoon and enjoy a peaceful life. Yet although they value the alternative of a traditional lifestyle, few seem to want to live there and the trend towards increasing urbanization continues. Thus, although the traditional island lifestyle has been retained as part of the Marshallese culture, and continues to exert an influence on the way they think, in practice a return to traditional lifestyles is not perceived as an option by many Marshallese. We now turn to an exploration of the impact of the Marshallese environment and culture on perceptions of health.

Chapter 9

Economic and Social Supports for Unhealthy Lifestyles

The reasons why people knowingly continue to do things which are injurious to their health are very complex, as discussed in Chapter 3. However, it is essential to attempt to understand them if effective health policy is to be formulated. This chapter focuses on the economic and social supports for unhealthy lifestyles. Our model of health dynamics in the Marshall Islands has value as a model that helps to explain the forces impacting on health behaviour in other countries. This chapter focuses on Marshallese perceptions of the nature of good health and the economic, cultural and environmental factors which determine Marshallese health. These perceptions, in turn, determine Marshallese health-related behaviour and the prevalence of lifestyle-related illness.

In a small Pacific country like the Marshall Islands, where traditional lifestyles were relatively healthy, it might be expected that good population health would be relatively easy to achieve. Certainly it would appear to be more difficult to achieve in larger and more complex peripheral countries. Earlier chapters in this book have established some similarities between the impact of global forces on the Marshall Islands and some other peripheral countries and marginalized groups. There are also similarities in the economic, social and cultural factors which support unhealthy lifestyles.

There are several dimensions to the perception of health. At the core is the image of what constitutes health and disease. To this must be added perceptions of what causes ill health, perceptions of ability or inability to influence these causes, and perceptions of appropriate methods to treat ill health. Western medical practitioners tend to assume that their patients share their view of what constitutes health and disease and also that, even if their patients do not understand the aetiology of a disease, they will accept and recognize the benefits of treatment. Yet images and perceptions of health vary markedly throughout the world. For example, obesity is variously perceived as a sign of fertility, wealth, prosperity, or completely the opposite, as a body shape strongly correlated with low socioeconomic status.[1] This can influence perceptions of the value of maintaining a medically defined 'ideal' bodyweight[2] in the interests of health, even among those who fully understand that obesity is a health risk factor.

Perceptions of disease are also complicated by different cultural orientations, and even when they are similar they do not necessarily result in the same behaviour in all societies. For example, a Chinese and a Western medical practitioner may have similar views about the causes of a condition such as an allergy, but may use different methods to treat it.[3]

People who believe a disease is caused by witchcraft or by some supernatural force are likely to treat it in a completely different way from those who believe it has more tangible causes, such as viral or bacterial infection, or nutrition. For example, in Pakistan some mothers living in slum communities believed that second and third degree malnutrition in their children was caused by witchcraft, and saw no connection at all with the amount of food the children consumed. This led them to treat malnutrition in ways which were ineffective and which even exacerbated the condition.[4]

Individual perceptions of ability to treat diseases are influenced not only by beliefs in the cause of disease but also by perceptions of general ability to influence life events. This broader view, which relates to attribution theory and how individuals perceive themselves in relation to the rest of the world, has been termed 'locus of control'.[5] People who believe in their own ability to take control of events and to solve problems are more likely to seek treatment for illness than are those who have a fatalistic view of the world. For example, many studies have shown that mothers with some education are more likely to take sick children to a health centre than are mothers with no education. There are various mechanisms through which education affects health behaviour, ranging from a greater understanding of health issues to facilitating greater control over resources and greater ability to seek care.[6] The effect, however, is that educated mothers are more likely to believe that they can do something to change or control their lives and the lives of their children.

Most cultures have specific images of health and perceptions of the causes of ill health. They relate to the health belief model and the perceived 'locus of control' as regards ability to treat ill health. Perceptions vary between cultures, and sometimes also between one region of a country and another or between socioeconomic groups.

This chapter is based on qualitative research in the Marshall Islands. It provides some important insights into Marshallese perceptions of health dynamics, and points to factors causing the high prevalence of lifestyle-related illness in the Marshall Islands. Some of these factors affect health and health perceptions in other peripheral societies, although people living in other societies may respond in different ways. The Marshallese data also provide a useful illustration of the way perceptions of health of some groups may be inconsistent with some of the assumptions which form the basis of the Western model of health care.

We used two main techniques to study Marshallese perceptions of health. One was a series of in-depth interviews which we carried out ourselves in Majuro with English speakers. Our respondents were many and varied, including health professionals, high school teachers and other educators, former peace corps volunteers, journalists, clerics, politicians, administrators, youth workers and various Marshallese who spoke English. The second method was a series of focus group discussions carried out in Majuro by Marshallese interviewers with other Marshallese, using the Marshallese language medium.

A male and a female Marshallese interviewer were employed to carry out focus group discussions with small groups of three or four men or women in three age groups: adolescent high school students, 30–40 year olds, and those aged 50 and over. The free-ranging focus group interviews covered various perceptions of health and ideal body weight; the main health problems in the Marshall Islands; the link between diet and health; the causes of poor diets; non-dietary causes of poor health; maternal and child health; and stress and social causes of ill health. Because we did not wish to hinder the flow of discussion by asking sensitive questions, and because our main interest was early-onset NCDs, the interviewers did not raise the topic of sexually transmitted diseases. However, focus group respondents spontaneously mentioned STDs and sexual behaviour from time to time as a health concern.

REASONS FOR UNHEALTHY LIFESTYLES IN THE MARSHALL ISLANDS

The explanation for health patterns can often be found in the characteristics, attitudes and experiences of populations. However, observers sometimes over-emphasize the importance of some of the most obvious characteristics of populations, and overlook the more important explanations. This is evident in the Marshall Islands and elsewhere in the Pacific where it is common to attribute the high prevalence of lifestyle-related illness primarily to specific characteristics and experiences, and to underestimate the impact on health of global political and economic forces. Interviews with Marshallese respondents indicated that generally specific characteristics and experiences were less important as causes of poor health than was uneven economic and social development. Some characterizations even appeared to be incorrect. The following pages first examine four particular characteristics and experiences that are over-emphasized, and then six factors which are more important causes of unhealthy lifestyles in the Marshall Islands.

Over-emphasized factors

1 Pacific people have different perceptions of health and beauty and they think ample body proportions are more desirable than a healthy weight
As discussed in Chapter 3, large body size is valued in many societies, and obesity has long been a symbol of high social status and prosperity in much of the Pacific, including the Marshall Islands. It does not automatically follow, however, that obesity is regarded as healthy or beautiful, or that this belief is a cause of the high prevalence of obesity in the Pacific region and constitutes an obstacle to the maintenance of a healthy bodyweight. Each group of Majuro respondents were shown sketches of men and women of different weights, equating roughly to ideal weight, 10 per cent overweight, 20 per cent overweight, 30 per cent overweight and 10 per cent underweight. In the sketches facial characteristics and

stance were depicted as uniformly as possible so that the only major difference between respondents was their bodyweight. They were asked to say which of the figures was the most healthy (ejmourtata) and which was the most attractive (emontata).

Generally respondents selected the figures with approximately ideal weight as both the healthiest and the most attractive, although there were some small differences of opinion among the men as to whether the figures who were about 10 per cent overweight might be more 'cuddly'. Only one woman in the 50 plus group selected an obese figure as the healthiest:

> Respondent One: *Well, some may say the man in the first picture is healthy because he is the fattest and others will say he is unhealthy because he is too fat.*
>
> Respondent Two: *Not the man in the first picture. He is too fat. And the man in the fifth drawing is not healthy because he is too thin.*
>
> Respondent One: *I still say the man in the first picture is the healthiest because he is big and fat.*
>
> Respondent Two: *I say the man in the third picture.*
>
> Respondent One: *The first woman looks big and healthy. And the second drawing is even better. Look at the size of her thighs! But the woman in the first drawing is the healthiest. The woman in the fifth drawing looks healthy too. But then we hear people saying people who are neither fat nor thin are healthy, so maybe the women in the third and fourth drawings are healthiest.*
>
> Respondent Three: *They are always telling us that we should lose weight, so, yes, maybe. They look like they might weigh the proper weight level – what is it, 125 pounds?*
>
> Interviewer: *And what is not an ideal weight?*
>
> Respondent Three: *140 pounds and over.*
>
> Respondent One: *That fat woman will have health problems because she is too fat.*
>
> Respondent Two: *Those two slim ones will not be burdened by their weight.*

These comments indicate that respondents generally had a sound perception of health, and most view excess weight as neither healthy nor attractive, especially among the younger age groups. It seems, however, that this is a change from the views held in the past, as indicated by the views of the older women and by the following exchange in the Women 30–40 group:

> Interviewer: *I'm sure you remember from your child-hood older people saying that someone who was healthy and prosperous was one who packed a few extra pounds. What are your thoughts on this?*
>
> Respondent: *Well, we have now discovered that this is not the case. We were misinformed. Nowadays, through education, we know that an overweight person may not be all that healthy. The same may apply to someone who is very thin.*

Thus, although obesity is still associated with high status, especially in older people, it is not necessarily perceived as healthy or attractive. As a symbol of status, rather than a factor defining status, obesity alone would not assist those who lack the rank and wealth to achieve high status.

In a subsequent interview a Marshallese woman commented that Marshallese and other Pacific men often tell their wives that they look better when heavier. She said this was not because they themselves liked fat women, but to ensure that their wives would not appear attractive to other men. A similar view was expressed by a Tongan woman. This suggests that being overweight and obesity are actually perceived as unattractive. Perceptions of ideal weight and health among the Majuro respondents, therefore, do not appear to be greatly at variance with medically defined ideal weight, and should not constitute an obstacle to the maintenance of a healthy bodyweight.

2 Pacific people do not know enough about major health problems and their causes; they need more health education, especially education in good nutrition
Each group was asked to name the main health problems in the Marshall Islands. The four adult groups – Men and Women aged 30–40 and 50 plus – all mentioned diabetes as the leading health problem in the Marshall Islands. The four adult groups also

mentioned cancer and thyroid problems. The Adolescent Girls and Women Aged 30–40 added kidney disease, heart disease, high blood pressure and complications of pregnancy to their lists of leading health problems. The Adolescent Boys also mentioned diabetes but focused on the lifestyle habits of smoking, drinking, chewing tobacco, marijuana and cocaine. This is a clear reflection of their own experiences and current concerns, as well as their currently low risk of developing the most prevalent NCDs.

A striking feature of the focus group discussions is that not one of the respondents mentioned an infectious disease as a leading health concern. Every condition discussed was non-communicable and, with the exception of pregnancy complications, strongly associated with lifestyle risk factors. This reflects widespread community awareness and concern about the high prevalence of early-onset NCDs as in the Marshall Islands. The unnecessarily high levels of such diseases, which are more likely to be an underlying than an immediate cause of death, is clearly attracting more attention than some of the leading immediate causes of deaths, such as pneumonia and sepsis (see Chapter 6).

Respondents were then asked their opinions about the causes of the health problems they had mentioned. All six groups of respondents ranked poor diets, and particularly the consumption of imported food, as a leading cause of poor health in the Marshall Islands. The Adolescent Boys and Men aged 30–40 mentioned smoking and drinking and a poor diet of 'ribelle' (foreign) food as major causes of such diseases, and the Adolescent Girls also mentioned pollution and stress. Most were eager to discuss dietary problems in detail, and had very strong views on the subject, as indicated in these comments by male and female respondents in the 30–40 year age groups:

> First Man aged 30–40: *I firmly believe that the major cause of diabetes is the type of food people consume today, especially on the urban centres such as Majuro, Ebeye, and to some extent, Jaluit. And the type I am referring to here is ribelle (foreign) food ... the food we import.*

> Second Man aged 30–40: *As a young man in the late 50s, I do not remember a single case of diabetes here in Majuro. Back then people's diets consisted largely of local food stuffs as there was only about one store on*

the whole island and a very limited shipping service. In comparison, today with development of all parts of our society and our money based economy, we consume mainly imported food items. And I have heard that 90 per cent of the patients in the hospital are diabetic. Don't you think there is a connection?[7]

First Woman aged 30–40: *Diseases are caused by our consuming food that is not good for us, which may result in such a disease as diabetes. Most important for a person's health is the right kind of food. Fatty foods, salty foods and sweet foods harm us. Fat, salt and sugar are the things that cause health problems in the Marshallese.*

Second Woman aged 30–40: *We consume too much sugar, especially those of us residing on the central islands who have no access to such traditional foods as coconut sap. Our diets consist mostly of rice, as we have very little access to our traditional foods. This is the main reason there is such a high number of diabetic cases today. We have chosen ribelle food over our own. We all know there is greater number of people with diabetes today than long ago.*

Male Respondent aged 30–40: *Food items such as corned beef, turkey tails, rice, sugar, and salt are harmful to us. But the way we prepare our food is also a factor. We all know that frying is a favourite Marshallese way of preparing meats of all types. Now we're being advised that excessive use of fat in the preparation of food, as well as consumption of fatty foods can lead to such health problems as diabetes.*

Woman aged 50 plus: *Our traditional food helped us in other ways too. For example, brushing one's teeth was taken care of by chewing pandanus. The fibres cleaned our teeth. So people long ago had healthy teeth. Nowadays, you see people who are still young who are wearing dentures. I personally believe people long ago were healthier because of the food they ate.*

The Women aged 50 plus attributed the generally better health of ribelles (foreigners) to their different diet, and drew some interesting comparisons:

Respondent One: *Ribelles are really healthy because they eat what is good for them, they eat the right kind of food. They have clean surroundings and eat at the proper times and eat the proper amount. Whereas, Marshallese eat anything, anytime, and in large, large amounts.*

Respondent Two: *Yes, all we eat is store bought. So we feel sick and unhealthy. It seems ribelles do not eat a lot of meat. They eat mostly greens.*

Respondent Three: *That's true. Things like cabbage. But we do not know how long most of the ribelle food we buy to eat has been stored so we cannot select the best quality. Besides they are not our foods so we do not know how to prepare them properly.*

Respondent Two: *Yes, ribelles know what goes well with what to get the most out of what they eat.*

It is clear from the comments of these Majuro residents that lack of dietary knowledge is not the main cause of high levels of NCDs. Respondents in all age groups were well aware that their general level of health is poor, and had a good understanding of the relationship of nutrition and health. However, a concerted nutrition education programme has effected little improvement in Marshallese diets. As discussed later in this chapter, socioeconomic factors play a much greater part in determining community health.

3 Marshallese attribute most of their health problems to nuclear testing and do not realize they are related to lifestyle
Another common explanation for the persistence of poor lifestyle habits in the Marshall Islands is apathy as a consequence of the extreme insults to community health inflicted by the nuclear testing programme. It is argued that this leads them to underestimate the contribution of their own lifestyle habits to NCDs such as diabetes and cardiovascular disease.

The effect of radiation on the health of those Marshallese who were exposed to nuclear testing is widely recognized, both officially and by the Marshallese population as a whole. There is no doubt that radiation has been a significant cause of NCD in the Marshall Islands, including various cancers and thyroid conditions, as discussed in Chapter 6. However, the focus group interviews indicated that generally respondents had a very good appreciation of which diseases were primarily a consequence of radiation and which were more closely associated with lifestyle. The four adult groups all mentioned radiation as a cause of disease, in each case they also mentioned the contribution of diet and lifestyle factors to NCDs, even those generally attributed to radiation. An example of their balanced view is this exchange in one of the male focus groups:

> First Male Respondent aged 30–40: *Besides the type of food we consume, I think some of the health problems we are experiencing today are a direct result of the nuclear tests conducted by the United States on Bikini and Enewetak. I know for a fact that a number of the major illnesses afflicting Marshallese today were non-existent before the testing programme. The Nuclear Claims Tribunal has drawn up a list of various cancers that fall under its compensation plan.*

> Second Male Respondent aged 30–40: *May I interrupt? While I agree that the nuclear tests may be a major factor in regards to health problems, I also would like to point out that the Division of Public Health informs us that such diseases as cancer are a result of cigarette smoking. So again, this is yet another indication that imported items play a significant part in people's health and well-being.*

The simultaneous appreciation of the very real and grave impact of radiation on Marshallese health, and also of the contribution of lifestyle factors to NCD is particularly well illustrated by the remarks of one woman in the 50 plus age group:

> *The ribelles contaminated our islands with their experiments, causing us to get cancer, thyroid, and other diseases. Another cause of the high rates of cancer and thyroid is our inability to buy the kinds of food that will not cause us to get these illnesses.*

In fact no hard evidence currently exists to demonstrate that diet can protect from, or reduce the risk of, radiation-related cancers, leukaemia and thyroid conditions. This respondent apparently assumed an association existed because she had been made very aware that a healthy diet greatly reduced the risk of developing diabetes.

One popular belief that constitutes a possible over-attribution of problems to radiation is that nuclear testing has caused coconuts and fruit to become stunted and produce less fruit:

> Woman aged 30–40: *Diseases such as cancer and thyroid are a result of these ribelles bombing our islands. The whole of the Marshalls is contaminated. And so you have people with thyroid, cancer; the direct result of poison from the bombs. Our flora are also affected, their growth is stunted; they too are contaminated. These are the problems.*

Although there is scientific evidence to indicate that coconut, pandanus and breadfruit in the northern atolls contain radioactive substances, including caesium 137,[8] ageing of trees is a more likely explanation for declining yields, as discussed in Chapter 4.

4 Pacific people have trouble staying thin because of 'the thrifty gene'

A fourth commonly offered explanation for poor Marshallese health relates to obesity. It is often argued that the Pacific physiology is distinctive in that it is better adapted to a feast–famine cycle because of 'the thrifty gene'. This particular genotype confers a survival advantage where marked fluctuations in food availability exist, such as in the traditional Pacific lifestyle. People with this gene, including most Pacific and Australian Aboriginal populations, are very efficient at storing nutrients in the form of fat reserves, which can be burned up when food intake decreases. Such people are thus more able to store nutrients during 'feast' periods and more able to survive 'famine' situations. This genotype becomes a disadvantage, however, when food availability tends to be more uniform, such as in a modern urban environment where there are no famines. Those who are efficient at storing nutrients store too much when exposed to a continual diet of high-fat, high-sugar, low-fibre food. If they never encounter periods of food shortage, the fat reserves simply accumulate and people then tend to become obese.[9]

Although there is strong evidence that the thrifty genotype contributes to Pacific obesity, the cause of obesity is eating patterns, not a specific genotype. The thrifty gene may make it more difficult for people to lose weight by restricting their food intake, but it does not prevent them from maintaining a healthy bodyweight if they adjust their eating habits. Substantial numbers of Marshallese are not overweight or obese, even though they share the same genetic heritage. It is also worth noting that improved metabolic efficiency can be developed by almost anyone who severely restricts their caloric intake. Weight lost in periods of semi-fasting is quickly regained when normal eating patterns are resumed, and it becomes increasingly difficult to shed weight solely by dieting.

It is thus evident that explanations which attribute high prevalence of NCDs in the Marshall Islands to particular genotypes and perceptions of health are limited and insufficient. In order to identify the main causes it is necessary to look at the broader political and economic setting, the impact of globalization on the Marshall Islands and the nature of Marshallese culture which shapes Marshallese response to these forces.

More important causes and supports for unhealthy lifestyles in the Marshall Islands

1 Urbanization without industrialization or substantial employment generation has resulted in displacement from the means of subsistence production coupled with widespread inability to purchase nutritious food
As discussed in Chapter 4, Majuro and Ebeye contain some 67 per cent of the total population of the Marshall Islands, but many residents rely on a share of the royalties from the American military presence or the income of employed relatives. According to the 1988 census, 13 per cent of Marshallese of working age were unemployed, and 79 per cent of the unemployed were aged 15–29 years. Many of the 25 per cent reporting as self-employed may have been under-employed. The employment situation has worsened since then as a result of population growth and recent public sector cutbacks. At the time of writing, unemployment on Majuro was probably in the vicinity of 20 per cent.

The most important cause of poor health habits identified by respondents related to their low incomes, separation from traditional lifestyles and displacement from the means of subsistence production. Low income groups are able to purchase only the cheapest food items. In the Marshall Islands this means white bread or polished white rice as the staple food, supplemented with low-grade fatty cuts of meat such as frozen turkey tails and spare ribs. The most popular, cheapest convenience foods, such as french fries, also tend to be laden with fat and low in food value. Sweet foods and carbonated drinks are available at low cost, whereas fruit and fruit juices, which are healthy substitutes for sugary food, are generally expensive. Perishables which are not produced locally, including meat, fresh fruit and vegetables, must be air-freighted to the Marshall Islands, so retailers sell them for high prices and stock only small quantities to minimize spoilage. Because of the absence of a local farming industry, low income families are generally unable to afford to supplement staples with healthy quantities of fresh fruit, vegetables and proteins.

> Man aged 30–40: *We not only consume only imported food stuffs, but are restricted to consuming only what we can afford. But now the information we are getting from the Ministries of Health and Social Welfare is that these types of food are not only non-nutritious, but can also lead to health problems if consumed in large amounts. But what are we to do if these are all we can afford?*

> First Woman aged 30–40: *Marshallese eat mainly rice, bread, chicken, beef, tuna, and other canned meats. These are the cause of our health problems today, the reason for so many types of illnesses. A typical Marshallese meal would consist of boiled rice, meat, and perhaps a pot of tea. Not many people would think or bother to add other food items such as cabbage or papaya. Sometimes it may be that they have not acquired a taste for cabbage and sometimes they cannot afford the cost of cabbage.*

> Second Woman aged 30–40: *Residing on Majuro prevents our having access to suitable traditional food. Sometimes traditional foods may be found in the stores, but we do not possess the financial means to purchase them. While prices in stores are continually going up, the minimum wage has remained constant. This is another problem. Now our government has been reducing the work force.*

First Woman aged 50 plus: *A place like Rita has no pandanus, very few coconuts and breadfruit trees. There are not enough places to grow these plants. People on the outer islands have healthy skins from the food they eat. But people on Majuro have scabies and other skin diseases and many are also night blind.*

Second Woman aged 50 plus: *So when we get sick we go to see the doctor and are told we need to eat cabbages and other greens to help us control our diabetes, but the problem is, where do we get the money to buy the cabbage and other greens? And where can one find space to plant on Majuro? If we were living on our own island, then we could plant a garden. People on the outer islands do not have as high a rate of diabetes and cancer as do we on Majuro, and they live longer.*

Third Woman aged 50 plus: *Even if you do have a place to grow these foods in Majuro, people steal what you plant. That's how much people realize our own foods are better for us than ribelle food.*

Urban poverty and displacement from the means of subsistence production is a worldwide phenomenon, particularly among groups marginalized by globalization. In almost every country populations who migrate to urban areas for various reasons, whether to find wage jobs, to share in the benefits of modernization or even simply to flee political unrest, are at risk of poor nutrition, substandard housing and unsanitary surroundings. Their capacity to live a healthy lifestyle is largely determined by their ability to earn a cash income. When incomes are low, they have no choice but to purchase the cheapest food, which tends to be the least nutritious. This is especially true in a country such as the Marshall Islands, where almost all of the food sold in urban areas is imported. In countries such as Uzbekistan, which produces substantial quantities of food, the urban poor are more likely to be able to afford an adequate diet, but they tend to be deficient in more expensive food, including meat and dairy produce.

2 The stress of urbanization without industrialization or employ-ment growth
Urbanization is also a leading cause of increased stress which promotes unhealthy lifestyles. In the poorer parts of urban Majuro and in Ebeye, settlements are dense and overcrowded.

> Adolescent Girl: *Houses are small and crowded together in Rita and Ebeye with many occupants and it's hard to get peace and quiet to study or sleep. Often you can't get to sleep because other people in the house or the neighbours are making a noise. Sometimes if we have male relatives around and we need to go to the toilet we will endure the discomfort until they are away from the bathroom entrance because it would be immodest to let them see you enter. I think we harm our health by suppressing a natural urge.*

Not only do such circumstances generate stress, but they also offer no outlets for it. Attempts to externalize feelings, such as by expressing anger, can lead to social conflict, whereas repression and internalization of anger increases personal stress. People who have no ready outlet for stress-induced feelings may overeat, smoke or drink alcohol as a way of expressing frustration. Domestic violence, including both spouse and child abuse, is also a symptom of stress. One of the main causes of stress in urban Marshalls is economic insecurity.

Budgetary assistance from the USA contributes more than 80 per cent of the Marshall Island's GDP.[10] Many people living in urban areas fear they could be severely affected if assistance is reduced substantially and there are further cutbacks in employment and a deterioration in economic conditions. Any cutbacks which occurred would be likely to impact much more severely on those living in urban areas than those in the outer islands who still have the opportunity to practise a subsistence lifestyle.

> Man aged 50 plus: *Living on the centres is difficult because you need money to survive. I cannot get what I need to survive if I do not have a job. And since I do not own the property I live on, if I want a coconut, I need money to buy it. Whereas, if I lived on my island I would not need money to survive. If you have only*

> *one person employed in say, a household of 15 people, about the only thing that person can buy is rice. A small amount can feed all members of the household. In order to buy better food, that person would have to earn more money.*

> Second Woman aged 50 plus: *Money, or the lack of it, is the root of all our social problems today. If people had enough money they would not have to worry so much and would be able to buy all the healthy and nutritious food their bodies require. This is why we have so many murder cases, especially among young, unemployed men. They may want something but do not have the means to obtain it so they get drunk and kill and rob someone, so they can buy whatever it is they want.*

Although there have been relatively few murders in the Marshall Islands in recent times, another symptom of extreme stress which has become prevalent is suicide. Between 1 October 1995 and 30 September 1996 there were 9 suicides and in 1994 there were 10, all committed by males.[11] They represented around 7 per cent of all male deaths in each year. Most of the theories about the high rates of suicide in Micronesia and elsewhere in the Pacific attribute them to stress and conflict caused by changes in the traditional social structure, or lack of opportunity for self-fulfilment.[12]

3 Retailing patterns and the promotion of foreign food by nutritionists and retailers

In the Pacific, nutrition has tended to be viewed mainly as a health issue and little attention has been paid to the availability of food and to linking nutrition with production and distribution.[13] However, retailing patterns and food availability are crucial determinants of health risk in the Marshall Islands where few people produce their own food.

The interaction between consumer demand and retailer supply is complex and circular. On the one hand consumers must have knowledge of available products before they exert a demand for them; on the other hand retailers must have an effective demand in order to sell a product. Small Pacific countries offer very limited markets to retailers, which tends to discourage them from stocking a wide variety of goods or introducing new goods which may not be assured of a market.

Food retailers in the Marshall Islands tend to stock a range of foods based on the American diet rather than on a traditional Pacific diet. This includes processed and packaged foods, white flour products, convenience foods, carbonated soft drinks and alcohol. Initially these foods were introduced to satisfy the demands of American military personnel resident in the Marshall Islands, and when the Marshallese acquired a taste for them retailers were happy to supply a larger market. Food aid also contributed to dietary change in the Marshall Islands. American-oriented nutrition programmes did not recognize the value of local foods such as green coconut milk, and encouraged the consumption of imported foods such as dairy produce and orange juice.[14]

Established retailing patterns are unlikely to change without a corresponding change in consumer preferences and effective demand, so it is difficult to introduce improvements to the Marshall Islands diet. In August 1997 one of the principal Majuro retailers began selling traditional foods at lunchtime on Fridays and Saturdays. He reported that this was popular and sales were good. However, the purchase price would have been beyond the means of poorer Majuro residents, and as sales were only intermittent, this activity was probably more in the nature of education and familiarization than a spearhead for dietary change.

As discussed above, respondents recognized the role of retailers and the profit motive in shaping not only their food preferences, but also the prevalence of drinking and smoking in the community.

> Woman aged 30–40: *Aren't cigarettes and alcohol two of the largest money-making imports today? Some people know that drinking and smoking is bad and yet persist in indulging. Maybe the parliament should pass a law banning the import of alcoholic beverages and cigarettes. It would not be bad and such a law would force people who use the two substances to stop.*

The question of whether Majuro residents would willingly reduce consumption of fat, sugar and salt and change to a healthier, traditional diet if they had the option is an interesting one. Although focus group discussions indicate that all age groups knew it would be healthier, preferences for imported foods are well established. Several informants mentioned that Majuro residents send store-bought food such as rice and canned beef to relatives on the outer islands because they believe they will be enjoyed. Also, as discussed in Chapter 4, children are fed on sweets and snack foods because some mothers believe that they must be good, because they are expensive and because children like them.

Majuro residents clearly enjoy high-fat, sweet and salty food. The standard fare served at restaurants and take-away outlets is very rich, typically comprising very large servings of fried fish or poultry, coleslaw and potato salad drenched in mayonnaise and white rice. Locally baked white bread is noticeably sweetened, and liberal amounts of sugar are normally added to hot beverages. Generally, there is not much variety in the type of food most commonly consumed. When preferences for such foods are so well established and people are generally unaccustomed to eating a wide range of foods, it is difficult to wean people away from rich diets. Attempts to do so must be very gradual so that taste preferences have time to adjust. The words of one respondent indicate how resistant Majuro citizens can be to the overzealous promotion of a traditional diet:

> Man aged 30–40: *I personally feel it is too late. We cannot very well advise people to revert back to a subsistence type economy. I mean, who would be willing to give up rice, corned beef, tea and sugar and go back to existing on breadfruit, fish and coconut water?*

The displacement of traditional diets by high-fat, high-sugar, high-salt Western foods constitutes a greater problem in the Marshall Islands than in marginalized countries which produce most of their own food. However, similar patterns can be seen among marginalized groups in developed countries, such as the Pima Native Americans, Australian Aboriginal communities and other low income groups in wealthier countries where the cheapest food options include processed, sugary, fatty and salty convenience foods. Although convenience food chains such as McDonald's have a presence in many developing countries, they tend to be relatively expensive compared with more nutritious local foods. For example, in Tashkent in 1997, cheap, nutritious food was readily available in the street market, while only those with higher incomes could afford processed and packaged food in supermarkets and the McDonald's-like hamburgers and chips retailed by the Bir fast-food chain. However, when general income levels rise so that convenience foods become cheaper than market foods, the poor are more at risk of adopting an unhealthy diet.

4 The nature of Marshallese culture

Marshallese culture, like most Pacific cultures, is communal, not individual. Marshallese place a particular emphasis on conformity. All socialization encourages children to bond with their peers and to avoid singling themselves out or becoming conspicuous. In Marshallese culture, as in virtually all cultures and certainly all Pacific cultures, food plays an important social function. On a day-to-day level families cook and eat together, and food sharing within families is important for group bonding. Providing food to the wider community at parties and celebrations is a demonstration of prestige which helps to define roles and bond communities.

One respondent remarked that one of the most unacceptable things a person can do in Marshallese culture is to hide food for their own consumption. He said that although he personally wanted to lose weight for health reasons it was very difficult for him because of family pressure to conform. As an unmarried male living with relatives he was expected to share their food and consume similar amounts to everyone else in the family. When he purchased special low-calorie food for himself he was considered to be selfish because the food was costly, even though neither he nor his relatives enjoyed this food. When he began to lose weight he was told he looked sick.

In the same way this cultural practice of eating together makes it difficult to prepare separate food for any household member, such as special food for children or pregnant women. A common manifestation in the Marshall Islands and elsewhere in the Pacific is under-nourished children and over-nourished adults.

The cultural practice of sharing food is echoed in the practice of sharing cigarettes, chewing tobacco and alcohol. Again, it would be antisocial for a Marshallese to refuse to participate and place individual health interests ahead of sociability. Although there are similar customs in American and other Western countries, the cult of individualism has made it acceptable for individuals to remain in a group without smoking, chewing or drinking.

Custom also affects physical activity. In Marshallese culture adults are expected to behave with dignity and decorum, especially women. This means slow movement and modest clothing.

Activities such as jogging along a roadside are acceptable in children, but considered inappropriate for Marshallese adults, especially for mature women. A woman in the 30–40 age group remarked:

> *People are not informed enough about the benefits of exercising. So some people may think that those who jog or walk are showing off, or worse, may make fun of those who jog, walk, or engage in other forms of physical exercise.*

The fact that jogging or walking could be interpreted as showing off, or a reason to make fun of someone almost certainly derives from the cultural emphasis on conformity and group rather than individual values. Anything that makes an individual conspicuous, could make them an object of attention and possibly even ridicule. A senior Marshallese government official confirmed this view, saying that Majuro residents take no notice when they see foreigners out jogging for health reasons, but when they see him doing it they stare in amazement and regard his behaviour as very odd.

Even so, in such societies the most effective health strategies need to be 'top down' approaches, in which leaders guide communities towards healthier behaviour by setting an example themselves. Such an approach to the promotion of weight loss has recently proved very effective in Tonga, a society with similar attitudes towards community and leadership. In that country the most esteemed member of the community, King Taufa'ahau Tupou the Fourth, participated in the national weight loss competition himself and shed 70 kg.[15] His involvement ensured the success of the campaign, and acceptance was such that a second national weight loss competition was launched in 1997.

Clearly, although Marshallese culture is similar to that of others in the Pacific, not all societies are organized in this way. The point to be made here is that culture is a source of support for unhealthy lifestyles, and strategies to modify health-related behaviour need to take culture into account. Issues such as whether a culture is communal or individualistic, whether there is gender equity, the way status is indicated, and ways in which a particular culture adapts to change and innovation, all need to be taken into consideration.

Another aspect of cultural appropriateness is taking into consideration matters such as dietary preferences. Along with the social role of food and the practice of communal cooking and eating, dietary preferences need to be taken into account in strategies to implement dietary change. For example, some nutritionists have promoted the replacement of white rice with brown rice into Marshallese diets, in an attempt to increase dietary fibre. Informants' opinions about the popularity of brown rice were mixed, and it seems that, like most Asian populations, Marshallese tend to prefer white rice. However, even if some members of a Marshallese household were to decide that they wish to eat brown rice, it would be considered unsociable for them either to compel the rest of the family to eat it, or to prepare separate food for themselves, especially given that the cost of brown rice is higher.

This means that strategies to improve Marshallese diets need to be very subtle. For example, rather than advocating total replacement of the white rice and bread-based diet by brown rice and traditional or health foods, it would be more acceptable to promote and facilitate the gradual addition of fibre and the gradual removal of fats and sugars. This might be achieved by blending and substituting either traditional or 'health' foods in the existing diet, and encouraging grilling rather than frying. Until this approach has been widely tried it is difficult to say whether Marshallese would willingly or easily give up their current high levels of consumption of fats, sugars and salt.

5 Perceptions of community and mortality

In the Marshall Islands, as elsewhere in the Pacific, community bonds are strong and community values are central to culture and daily life. Whereas modern Western society tends to promote individualism rather than community values, in Pacific societies it is socially unacceptable to place individualism ahead of community values. This perception may also influence health behaviour. Most Marshallese are practising Christians who believe the soul is immortal and that those who have lived a good life will one day be reunited with their families in Heaven. This, along with the belief that God cares for his flock may encourage passivity as regards self-care.[16]

Moreover, the Christian churches teach that those who go to Heaven will be free of the troubles and suffering of life on earth. In a communally oriented society these basic Christian beliefs tend to support the attitude that it is more important to nurture community bonds which will endure beyond death, than to adopt an individual view. Death itself may be perceived not so much as an end but as a transition to a better place. This greatly reduces the fear of death, and makes it less important to take individual action to be healthy in order to avoid an early death, but very important to observe community values and maintain a secure place in one's community. In this context it would appear foolish to risk alienating the community by behaving in a socially unacceptable way, such as by refusing food and drink or moving in an undignified fashion, simply to avoid an early death.

More research is needed to assess the effect of community values and religious beliefs on individual health behaviour in the Marshall Islands and other societies. However, it may be an important factor in relation to obesity and lifestyles, especially among those groups in any society who hold the strongest religious beliefs. For example, some women living in Pacific communities in Wellington, New Zealand, have indicated that their perception of community and death makes it unimportant for them to reduce weight and improve fitness levels in the interests of individual longevity.[17] It is possible that similar views may prevail among some Marshallese, especially among older men and women.

6 Assessment of personal health risks

In both developed and developing countries many people have a poor understanding of the causes of disease, and do not appreciate the direct links between unhealthy behaviour and NCD. This does not seem to be the case in Majuro, where interview respondents generally demonstrated a sound appreciation of the causes of NCD. This indicates that health education programmes are effective and are reaching their target audience. However, in Majuro, as elsewhere, knowledge alone is not sufficient to prevent people engaging in unhealthy lifestyle habits.

One reason for this is that even if people understand the adverse health consequences of some behaviours, they may assess their personal risk as low. A cause of underestimation of personal risk is that NCDs such as cancer, heart disease and diabetes, tend to take many years to develop, and even then they do not affect everyone who is at risk. Hence the connection between unhealthy behaviour and disease is not very direct. It has been estimated that smoking reduces life expectancy at age 20 by 7 minutes per cigarette. Consumption of five alcoholic drinks in a day is estimated to reduce life expectancy at age 20 by an hour, and each drink in excess of five reduces it by a further 20 minutes.[18]

Most drinkers and smokers indulge for many years before they develop lung cancer, and some smokers never do. Similarly, consumption of large amounts of alcohol, and a diet too rich in fats and sugars does not have an instantaneous impact on health. This does not mean that the statistics are incorrect; but rather that they refer to average risk and not to a definite outcome. We can conjecture that it would be a very different scenario if the connection between unhealthy behaviour and disease were more direct, such as if all smokers developed lung cancer one week after they smoked their first packet of cigarettes. Since this is not so, it can be very difficult to use risk arguments to persuade people to abandon activities which give them pleasure. This is especially true in a culture such as the Marshall Islands where social interaction is important and where eating, drinking and smoking are part of sociable behaviour.

Marshallese who are well informed about the health risks attached to certain behaviours do not necessarily modify their behaviour. Like people everywhere in the world, if it is difficult to give up a certain behaviour and there is not strong support from family and friends to do so, they persuade themselves that they will be one of the lucky ones who escape the negative consequences. On the other hand, people who have been pushed into retreatist behaviour by adverse economic and social circumstances, may continue with a deleterious behaviour even when they are well aware of the risk. In such cases deliberately self-destructive behaviour, such as drinking to excess, may occur regardless of individual perception of risk. Such behaviour is evident not only in the Marshall Islands, but in many other peripheral countries and marginalized groups throughout the world.

SUMMARY

Discussions with Marshallese residents make it clear that the major forces shaping health-related behaviour in the Marshall Islands are related more to the impact of globalization than to any unique characteristics of the Marshallese themselves. The Marshallese experience of urbanization without industrialization or substantial employment generation is the underlying factor affecting health and the high prevalence of NCDs in Majuro and Ebeye. At the same time, the health of residents of the outer islands is affected by the underdevelopment of the country as a whole.

The globalization of the Marshall Islands has led to displacement from the means of subsistence production, coupled with widespread inability to purchase nutritious food. It is also a cause of stress and social disruption. The peripheral location of the Marshall Islands as regards the US superpower is the major determinant of the lifestyle options available to Marshallese, and their culture has determined their choices from the available options. The Marshallese experience parallels that of other countries which have been made peripheral by global forces. Although perceptions and responses may differ, the forces shaping them are essentially the same.

Chapter 10

Conclusion

This study has examined the impact of globalization on health. In particular it has been concerned with the manner in which the widespread adoption of a liberal capitalist model of development has led to increasing disparities of wealth. Those denied the benefits of economic growth, including improved health care, have been marginalized, and this in turn has negative effects on their health.

The factors which determine lifestyles and health behaviour are extremely complex. In order to understand them it is necessary to take a multidisciplinary approach which considers the geographical and environmental context, the nature of culture and society, local politics and economics, international relations and global politics and economics. Although there are common themes, each society experiences a unique blend of these factors and has its own unique responses. Our case studies of Mongolia, Uzbekistan and the Marshall Islands illustrate the ways in which these factors interact to shape lifestyles and health. Similar studies are needed in other societies to identify the causal factors shaping their lifestyles and health.

MODERNIZATION AND HEALTH

The processes of demographic and health transition which most modern industrialized countries experienced in the 19th and early 20th centuries have not been replicated in countries on the periphery of the global political economy. It can be argued that certain communities and individuals have been deliberately disadvantaged by the processes of modernization and globalization. There has been a continuing flow of economic wealth from the periphery to the core, both within countries and internationally. While it is possible to demonstrate an overall increase in international trade and subsequent generation of wealth, not all people have benefited from this growth. Some development theories contend that economic growth must be the forerunner of poverty alleviation, but current trends suggest that, although growth is occurring, it is not having the expected 'trickledown' effect. In particular, patterns of poverty and ill health demonstrate a very uneven experience of development across societies all over the world.

As demonstrated in this study, there are distinct characteristics to the spheres of politics and economics, despite significant overlapping. In theory, the political realm of governance has an obligation to meet basic needs. At present this obligation resides with national government, although some international assistance occasionally may be forthcoming. Each of the country examples presented here are facing difficulties meeting basic needs from domestically generated funds. Even if there were political will to address such needs, the liberal capitalist model of economic development impedes such policies.

The emergence of a global political economy reflects a number of interactions which have developed a global dimension. The free flow of capital coordinated by powerful multinational corporations and economic institutions, environmental impacts on a global scale and a widespread acceptance or imposition of liberal capitalism have all contributed to growing socioeconomic disparities. Despite this, globalization is a limited process in that issues of economics which have taken on significant global dimensions are not reflected to a similar degree in the realm of politics.

MODERNIZATION, GLOBALIZATION AND SOCIETY

Although many aspects of domestic civil society are now influenced by international and global issues, there has been very specific and limited extension of civil society principles to the international and global levels. Even the United Nations Universal Declaration on Human Rights is far from universally interpreted or upheld. Similarly, the provision of basic needs is recognized as a potential 'shared good' in political pronouncements, but not seriously addressed by the international community. Although valuable work is undertaken by relevant UN agencies and non-governmental organizations, at present the development of a global society appears to be limited to issues of economics and how various groups and individuals benefit or are marginalized within this process.

Despite the establishment of the WTO and attempts at coordinating global trade and commerce, such an approach has not been extended to other areas of human interaction and governance. Even the UN is little more than a collection of member states with extremely limited powers to act as a global polity. Authority tends to be seen as residing at the level of individual states with national sovereignty remaining paramount. Clearly increased interdependence, the spread of modernization and the emergence of global issues has challenged this concept. However, with the exception of matters of international trade, there is scant coordination to address issues such as the provision of basic needs and environmental degradation. Summit conferences are held, but apart from severely limited overseas aid programmes, little has been done to counter the detrimental impacts of the poverty associated with the dominant model of liberal capitalism. Without a holistic approach that coordinates individual governments at the international level, marginalization is likely to continue.

It is significant that Mongolia and Uzbekistan fall into a 'catch all' category of what have been described as 'economies in transition'. The Marshall Islands could come to be described in this way if it loses the support of US funding. However, a more holistic approach would be to describe these three states, and many others affected by modernization and globalization, as 'societies in transition'. Under this rubric the Marshall Islands could be included as there has been significant societal change, even though the Marshallese have maintained the essential elements of their traditional culture. Similar cultural tensions and evolutions are happening on a global scale. These broader aspects feed into the behavioural patterns that shape lifestyle choices. As described in Chapter 9, the prevalence of early-onset NCDs and other health issues are closely related to a broad range of domestic and international socioeconomic factors.

Many of the UN member states provide aid programmes to developing states or contribute to disaster relief funds. Again these can be seen as curative measures. In essence they are adding water to a leaking bucket as opposed to fixing the hole. Some natural disasters may be seen as beyond human control. However, many other aspects of poverty and depravation can be more closely linked to social constructs and processes. In particular this relates to global economic institutions and the manner in which they facilitate uneven development.

MODERNIZATION, GLOBALIZATION AND LOCAL CONTROL

One of the key reasons for focusing on preventive rather than curative development policies is to allow greater participation at the community level. Proponents of modernization suggest that people who are able to benefit from liberal capitalism have greater freedom and opportunity. For some people this may be true, but in terms of having control over economic decision making the key elements of this process have been increasingly centralized and determined by small groups of governments and multinational corporations. By refining the process of international trade, an elite group of states and multinational corporations have effectively taken control over expanding networks of economic interactions which have far-reaching impacts on the world's population. For many people, if longer-term environmental consequences are discounted, their living standards have improved. However, the reverse is true for those marginalized from such benefits. This applies in both the industrialized and developing worlds. Where aid to these groups has been forthcoming it has been to offset the damage caused by the process of marginalization. To administer more appropriate preventive measures requires a degree of decentralization or, at least, a greater understanding and accommodation of more localized factors.

Focusing at the local level immediately makes it clear who is in greatest need and what measures are appropriate in a particular circumstance. It might be the case that the cause of inequality or suffering is based some distance away and will need to be dealt with at its source. However, at least in the short term, it is necessary to have a clear understanding of how a problem manifests, and what response would be most successful in any given cultural setting. For example, the use of traditional medicine, previously suppressed in Mongolia, is being regenerated as it is viewed as more culturally appropriate than some other forms of health care.

This type of approach is at the heart of the Local Agenda 21 network that has evolved as part of the Earth Summit process. In stark contrast to the largely ineffective attempts at intergovernmental environmental negotiations, such as the Kyoto summit on climate change, the devolved, locally focused approach has given rise to optimistic forecasts for more equitable and sustainable development policies. Although the spread of Local Agenda 21 groups has to date been largely restricted to the developed states, the principle could usefully be applied throughout the world.

The basic principle of Local Agenda 21 is to involve a broad range of individuals and groups drawn from across a community. These will involve local government officials, business people and a broad array of non-governmental organizations, including women's groups and other interest groups. Local environmental and community concerns are addressed with an appreciation of the global forces bearing on them. An awareness of these connections is the first step towards countering their negative impacts. In particular, this relates to adopting a coordinated approach to the alleviation of poverty and other factors that contribute to ill health. The extent to which change can be effected varies between areas, and in relation to the vested interests in operation. For example, it is unlikely that a small community group will have much impact on the world market price of a particular commodity. However, it could have a much greater impact in terms of drawing a community together, improving local facilities and building a stronger sense of community spirit to facilitate more effective lobbying within external arenas. Such lobbying may be directed towards national governments, international organizations or multinational corporations via coordinated consumer boycotts or positive purchasing.

The example of Local Agenda 21 illustrates the scope for locally coordinated reversal of the negative aspects of economic marginalization. Given the extent and power of interests operating within the global political economy, there will be occasions where local resistance will be unsuccessful, or even futile. However, only by collectivization can marginalized groups and individuals promote their interests effectively. One of the greatest obstacles with regard to collectivization is the disempowerment which often comes with marginalization. By definition, those at the margins of socioeconomic interactions are in a poor position to effect change.

Another aspect of the Local Agenda 21 approach is that it highlights the benefits of a coordinated, holistic strategy. By involving as broad a range of interest groups as possible, these forums are able to air differing points of view and often enable impromptu conflict resolution. In each of the societies this study has considered there is scope for such a forum. One of the key characteristics of the experience of modernization in these, and other, societies is that various actors develop differing interests and agendas. Clearly some differences would have existed in pre-modernized societies. However, as disparities become more apparent, so, too, do potential conflicts of interest. While not guaranteeing a solution to all such conflicts, locally based forums at least offer the possibility of a managed reduction in conflict, and could facilitate mutually acceptable compromises.

Although there is some cause for optimism in relation to conflict resolution at the local level it is much harder to achieve at the global level. The greatest disparities of wealth cross state boundaries. This is not only in terms of particular individuals but also on a societal scale. Examples are the disparities in relative consumption per capita of mineral resources and wastes arising from mass consumerism. Localized approaches to equity and sustainability can only achieve so much. They are unlikely to extend to seriously redressing the global imbalance in health, wealth and well-being. Such a task will require a coordinated international approach. Almost certainly this would involve a fundamental reassessment of the benefit of economic growth and the manner in which it is currently generated. Despite some clear benefits of modernization, there are many partially hidden costs in terms of environmental degradation, and the negative experiences felt by those on the margins of the global political economy.

POSSIBLE FUTURES

This study has highlighted the inequalities that arise via modernization. Assuming current patterns of modernization and globalization continue, what possible futures are there for the states focused on here and, by implication, broader international relations?

Despite an abundance of accessible resources, Mongolia and Uzbekistan have faced more socioeconomic challenges in recent years than has the Marshall Islands. Although it has faced significant ill health and other related problems and the longer-term prospects remain uncertain, the Marshall Islands has retained significant funding from the USA. In stark contrast, the other two states have had to make rapid adjustments to the collapse of the Soviet Union, a resulting loss of subsidies and the need to adapt to a competitive international economic environment. A similar fate may yet await the Marshallese but there is hope that the USA will facilitate a smoother transition than occurred in Eastern Europe and Central Asia.

The resource base available to Mongolia and Uzbekistan should aid their economic recovery. Structural adjustment programmes and foreign direct investment demonstrate that there is engagement with the international economy. Issues such as the environmental degradation surrounding the Aral Sea region will partially offset economic growth in Uzbekistan, but such growth is likely to occur. Similarly, Mongolia has sufficient resources and is well placed geographically to supply markets in Russia and, increasingly, the demand from a growing Chinese economy. The potential for economic growth far outweighs the negative impact of withdrawal of Soviet sponsorship. What is less clear is the extent to which both Mongolia and Uzbekistan can ensure that the benefits of growth can be utilized to prevent further marginalization of disadvantaged groups. The communist ideological legacy in these states should go some way towards ensuring, at least, an attempt to meet the basic needs of the respective populations.

It is a popular myth that the rejection of many of the governments within the former Soviet Union represented a wholesale rejection of socialist principles. Although there will obviously be individual differences, particular regimes were rejected because they were failing to keep to these principles, not because of their espousal of Soviet ideology. Despite the widespread adoption of free market economics, the popular will to meet such needs remains in the former Soviet Union and its satellite states, although this does not necessarily guarantee success. With economic advisers from the World Bank and the IMF operating within both Mongolia and Uzbekistan, there will be little support for increasing welfare provision at the expense of investment in longer-term projects geared towards national economic growth. Again this reflects the dominance of curative as opposed to preventive economic policies that do not immediately address basic needs.

Both Mongolia and Uzbekistan are likely to face higher rates of lifestyle-related diseases as they emulate patterns associated with modernization. Changes in diet, patterns of exercise, residence and possible stress-related factors are all likely to contribute to increased ill health unless they are paralleled by the motivation and opportunity to adopt healthier lifestyles.

In contrast to Uzbekistan and Mongolia, the Marshall Islands faces somewhat different problems and prospects. Although the Marshall Islands is disadvantaged in a number of market opportunities, none is insurmountable. The fundamental requirement for taking control of developments in the Marshall Islands relates to the willingness of the government to engage more positively with both its economic and political international environment. Although this book generally emphasizes the impact of overseas contact on the Marshall Islands, the effect of outside contact need not be a wholly passive experience. Already, licensing deals have shown how much potential wealth there is in the Marshall Islands and its marine environs. If these were to be developed locally the prospects for the Marshall Islands' economy would improve tremendously. How this might come about is essentially a political issue.

The Marshall Islands' economic survival will be a matter of degree. It will be judged on various performance indicators and will doubtless have mixed impacts on the population. Economic benefits or costs are rarely, if ever, meted out equally across societies. Political survival is somewhat different as it impacts, at least initially, on ruling parties. To date the Marshallese government has bridged the gap between traditional and modern society by integrating the chiefly system and the newer parliamentary system. Economic changes, for better or worse, are inevitable, but it is less clear how these will impact on the political system. Issues such as land tenure retain great importance in Marshallese society and it is difficult to see how this would ever alter. The evolution of the Republic was overseen by the chiefly system and the elite Kabua clan, and because of this link there remain strong cultural sentiments that work in favour of the ruling party. This has not been challenged, in part, because some basic needs have been met and there has been insufficient support for any significant opposition. This may not continue if the current economic recession has a greater negative impact on more of the population.

Political survival in the Marshall Islands will need to rely on more than respect for tradition. There are already more vocal criticisms of government policy than in previous years. The death of the first President, Amata Kabua, in 1996 presented an opportunity for reassessment of the government. Although he was replaced by another member of the Kabua family, there is the sense that one era has passed and the next phase of the Marshall Islands' development is yet to be determined. Although other factors will play a role in this development, economic issues will be fundamental.

With respect to the longer-term economic future of the Marshall Islands, much depends on the outcome of any future renegotiation of the relationship with the USA. If US funding were to be radically reduced this could prompt further economic crises, with the likelihood of increased marginalization for those already economically disadvantaged with a resulting negative impact on health. Depending on individual circumstances, some Marshallese may choose to leave the islands, perceiving greater opportunities overseas. The option to do this will depend on the individual's level of education or whether he or she has relatives living abroad. Others may choose to return to more traditional lifestyles, perhaps based on one of the outer islands. Alternatively, such a development could lead to a more proactive approach to independent economic growth. Regardless of which future scenario occurs the issue of NCDs and general health care provision will require a holistic understanding and approach to meeting ongoing demands.

A common weakness of health policy is a tendency to take too narrow a view of health problems. The origins of this are clear. In the pre-health transition stage, when infectious diseases are the main concern, broad-brush medical and hygiene interventions are the best approach to reducing mortality. This changes, however, as environmental conditions improve and lifestyle-related diseases become the main health concern. Responsibility for health gradually shifts to the individual, and broad-brush interventions become less important than the lifestyle options available and the choices made. When this point is reached there is no medical 'quick-fix' for health problems; instead a way of improving health-related behaviour is needed, and a way of influencing the determinants of this behaviour.

In recent decades the primary health care initiative has, to some extent, moderated the purely medical approach to health care by emphasizing the importance of cultural relevance and community involvement, and by stressing the need for health education. Even so, there is still a tendency for governments to pigeon-hole health concerns as primarily within the domain of health departments, perhaps with some assistance from social services, public works and education. Insufficient emphasis has been given to the multi-causal nature of health problems, and particularly to global impacts on health and lifestyles. As a consequence, the crucial point is often overlooked: health improvement is too complex and too large a task to be left to health departments; it must be tackled as a societal concern, both domestically and internationally.

Health education policies in the Marshall Islands have been shown to be successful in terms of spreading information. Interview respondents demonstrated a high level of understanding regarding nutrition, the value of exercise and the negative effects of over-consumption of alcohol and tobacco. A certain degree of 'blame shifting' was in evidence with respondents, who were more likely to identify external causes for ill health rather than accepting that they had a higher degree of control over their health than they wished to admit. Despite this attitude there was also evidence that, indeed, there were factors relating to ill health that were apparently beyond the immediate control of individuals. These related to a dependent economy, under-developed resource base, poor infrastructure and general economic vulnerability due to geographic situation and disadvantaged trading opportunities.

The case of the Marshall Islands demonstrates clearly that health education does not necessarily improve health behaviour. No matter how well people understand what is good for them and what is bad for them, their lifestyles are still determined primarily by what is culturally appropriate, what resources are available to them and what is possible in their local and global setting. When these underlying factors are not conducive to the pursuit of healthy lifestyles, health education campaigns are likely to have little effect. All too often the promotion of health is left to a few government departments, which are unable to influence the underlying determinants of lifestyle. In such circumstances they may be able to achieve little, but, in the words of a senior Marshallese health official, 'what else can I do but keep bombarding the people with health education and hope that eventually they change?'.

Recognizing problems is only the first step towards solving them. In terms of survival strategies it may be that the Marshall Islands and other peripheral states will have to lower their expectations of what they can achieve. This is not to consign vast numbers of the developing world to a future without hope of improvement in living standards and other elements of well-being. Rather it is to highlight that current strategies for development tend to promote inequality. A more holistic view of what constitutes overall development is needed, as opposed to one which favours some, but marginalizes others.

At the beginning of this study health was defined as 'a state of complete physical, mental and social well-being, not merely the absence of disease or infirmity'. It is apparent that the liberal capitalist model of development is denying health to many, by promoting unequal access to resources and health care. It also is reducing their prospects of achieving physical, mental and social well-being, and promoting uneven progress in health. Pursuit of economic growth has become a goal divorced from societal needs. It has failed to extend to all groups the full range of available options from which lifestyle choices are made. Economic growth needs to be managed in order to promote equitable and sustainable development and allow everyone the opportunity to enjoy a healthy lifestyle.

Notes

CHAPTER 1

1 Beck, 1994
2 Wallerstein and Hopkins, 1996; Myrdal, 1953; Frank, 1978
3 Chomsky, 1993; Buchanan, 1985
4 Robertson, 1992
5 Tomlinson, 1991
6 UNDP, 1997b: 38
7 ibid
8 Cox, 1987; Strange, 1996
9 Frank, 1978
10 Keohane and Nye, 1987
11 Chomsky and Herman, 1988
12 Fukuyama, 1992
13 Hagen, 1962
14 Merton and Chirot, 1986
15 Omran and Strandley, 1976
16 Diamond and McDonald, 1994: 32
17 Durkheim, 1986
18 Brown and Harris, 1989
19 Collis, 1997: 21
20 Hetzel and McMichael, 1987: 31

CHAPTER 2

1 Timberlake, 1985: 82–6
2 UNDP, 1997b: 3
3 Brandt and the Independent Commission on International Development Issues, 1980
4 Brown, 1974
5 Timberlake, 1985: 72–3
6 UNFPA, 1997

7   Report of the Independent Commission on Population and Quality of
    Life, 1996: 98

Chapter 3

1   United Nations, 1982
2   Hart et al, 1990: 9
3   Calculated from UNICEF, 1996a: 80–1
4   UNDP, 1996b, 1997
5   UNDP, 1997b: 53–5
6   Eg Black et al, 1982; Marmot and Wadsworth, 1997; Marmot and
    Wilkinson, 1999
7   Eg United Nations, 1982; Preston, 1989; Millard et al, 1990
8   UNICEF, 1996a: 95
9   UNFPA, 1997: 30
10 Khan et al, 1989
11 Rusman, 1999: 64
12 Anderson and Staugard, 1986
13 UNICEF, 1994: 43
14 See the quotation at the head of Chapter 1
15 Hart et al, 1990: 9–10
16 Caldwell, 1989
17 Royston and Armstrong, 1989
18 Becker et al, 1977
19 King, 1983
20 For a fuller discussion of these theories see Simons, 1989
21 Raharjo and Corner, 1990: 526–7
22 Hodge et al, 1996: 81
23 de Garnie and Pollock, 1995
24 Manning et al, 1991: 62, 86
25 Ender, 1988: 46; Harpham, 1994
26 Ender, 1988; Cohen et al, 1986
27 Ashton and Stepney, 1982
28 Zuckerman, 1988
29 Department of Environment, Sport and Territories, 1995
30 Spielberger et al, 1988: 94
31 United Nations, 1996
32 Derived from responses to various surveys carried out by DHS, Macro
    International, Columbia, Maryland, 1987–1996

Chapter 4

1   Onon and Pritchatt, 1989: 5
2   ibid: 7

3   Rupen, 1979: 23
4   ibid: 52–3
5   ibid: 1981–82
6   Jagchid and Hyer, 1979: xiii
7   Neupert, 1996
8   Griffen (ed), 1995:15
9   ibid: 12
10 OECD, 1996: 21
11 Griffen (ed) 1995, 19; UNDP, 1996a
12 Briguglio, 1995
13 Cited in Peace Corps Volunteers, 1986: 15
14 Cameron, 1987: 196
15 Bushnell, 1993
16 Heine, 1974: 13
17 Peattie, 1992; Purcell, 1976
18 Smith, 1997: 43–51
19 Marshall Islands Government, 1995
20 Weisgall, 1994
21 *Washington Pacific Reporter*, April 1997: 6
22 Berg, 1988
23 Eknilang, in Clark and Sann, 1996: 242
24 *Pacific News Bulletin*, Feb/March 1988: 5

Chapter 5

1   IMF, 1992: 9
2   ibid: 11
3   ibid: 16
4   Neupert, 1995
5   Centre for Co-operation with the Economies in Transition, 1996: 11
6   ibid: 20
7   Cited in ibid: 27
8   ibid: 32
9   IMF, 1992: 3
10 OECD, 1996: 11
11 UNDP, 1996a
12 World Bank, 1993
13 Chapman, 1989
14 Marshall Islands Government, 1996a: 60
15 ibid: 76
16 Rosenstrater, 1996
17 Sprout, 1985

CHAPTER 6

1   Mongolian Government, 1994
2   ibid: 37
3   UNICEF, 1996a: 80; UNDP, 1997c: 16
4   Mongolian Government, 1994: 134; UNICEF, 1996a: 80
5   UNDP, 1997c: 16
6   UNICEF, 1996a: 92; UNDP, 1997c: 17
7   The basis for the official projections is not shown in Mongolian Government (1994), but this information was communicated to one of the authors by State Statistical Office staff
8   Cariceo, 1994: 104
9   ibid, 112
10 Mongolian Government, 1993
11 Medvedeva, 1996: 187–90
12 ibid: 88
13 Medvedeva, 1996: 178
14 UNDP, 1997c: 17
15 Mongolian Government, 1993
16 Neupert, 1995: 44–5
17 Cariceo, 1994: 70
18 Neupert, 1995: 45
19 UNDP, 1997c: 17
20 Cariceo, 1994: 108
21 ibid: 109
22 Mongolian Government, 1993: 125. Calculated as current expenditure in Mongolian tugrigs adjusted to prevailing US$ exchange rate
23 UNDP, 1997c: 36
24 Griffen et al, 1994, cited in Medvedeva, 1996: 184
25 UNDP, 1997c: 28
26 Kachondham 1992: 39
27 Cariceo, 1994: 70
28 Cariceo, 1994: 102
29 Calculated from UNDP, 1997c: 22
30 UNDP, 1997c: 22
31 UNICEF, 1990: 6
32 Kachondham, 1992: 12
33 ibid: 25
34 UNDP, 1997c
35 UNDP, 1995: 47; UNDP, 1996a: 99
36 DHS, 1996: 6.
37 ibid
38 UNDP, 1995: 47
39 UNDP, 1996a: 108
40 ibid: 93
41 Goskomprognostat, 1995

42 ibid: 47
43 ibid: 99
44 World Bank, 1993
45 UNDP, 1995: 37
46 UNDP, 1995: 36
47 ibid
48 UNDP, 1995: 52
49 ibid: 54–5
50 ibid: 42
51 ibid: 43
52 ibid: 79
53 See, for example, UNDP, 1995: 41
54 ibid: 43
55 UNDP, 1996a: 61
56 ibid: 35
57 Hetland and Haycock, 1995: 120
58 Ordnung, 1996:25–26
59 UNDP, 1995: 36
60 UNDP, 1996a: 62
61 UNDP, 1995: 36
62 ibid
63 DHS, 1996: 10
64 ibid: 8
65 UNDP, 1995: 49
66 UNDP/ILO, 1995
67 UNDP, 1996a

CHAPTER 7

1 See McArthur, 1967; Bushnell, 1993
2 Finsch, 1893: 11
3 ibid: 46
4 ibid: 12
5 Marshall Islands Government, 1988: 14
6 ibid
7 Marshall Islands Government, 1989
8 Marshall Islands Government, 1994: 25
9 Marshall Islands Government, 2000
10 Marshall Islands Government, 1989: 93
11 ibid
12 Marshall Islands Government, MOHE, 1996: 60
13 Marshall Islands Government, 1989: 22
14 Smith, 1997
15 The 1988 census reported 67 per cent living in urban areas (Marshall Islands Government, 1989)

16   ibid: 17
17   Kramer, 1906: 78–80
18   ibid: 205
19   ibid: 83
20   Murai, 1954: 2–7
21   ibid: 9
22   ibid: 169, 226–35
23   ibid: 79
24   Marshall Islands Government, 1991: 47–53
25   ibid: i–v
26   Coyne et al, 1984: 45
27   Booth, 1989: 11
28   Ministry of Health and Environment Annual Report FY96 (draft), Marshall Islands Government, MOHE, 1997: 38
29   D Scrimgeour, personal communication, November 1997
30   Marshall Islands Government, MOHE, 1996
31   Pietrzik, 1991
32   WHO, 1990: 11
33   See various papers collected in de Garnie and Pollock, 1995
34   Hodge et al, 1996: 77
35   ibid: 78, 79, 81
36   ibid: 55
37   ibid: 55
38   Pollock, 1995: 95
39   ibid: 56
40   ibid: 56
41   Jamie W Spence, Canvasback Missions, personal communication
42   de Garnie and Pollock, 1995: 57
43   Hodge et al, 1996: 82
44   Schoeffel, 1992: 241
45   Schoeffel, 1992: 240
46   ibid: 58
47   Jamie W Spence, Canvasback Missions, personal communication
48   Marshall Islands Government, MOHE, 1996: 58 and 1997: 25A
49   McMurray, 1995
50   Collins et al, 1996: 89
51   Marshall Islands Government, 1990, 1994
52   Marshall Islands Government, 1990: 63
53   Marshall Islands Government, MOHE, 1996: 37
54   Nuclear Claims Tribunal, 1996b: 18.
55   Annual report on Compact, Marshall Islands Government, 1996a: 63
56   See, for example, Ruvussin et al, 1994; Australian Institute of Health and Welfare, 1996
57   UNDP, 1995: 36

CHAPTER 8

1   Soucie, 1983: 12–5
2   ibid: 30–2
3   Pollock, 1974: 110
4   Marshall Islands Visitors Authority, 1997: 45
5   ibid
6   See discussion in Pollock, 1974
7   Carucci, 1997: 97
8   ibid: 97
9   Johnson, cited in UNICEF, 1996.
10 Marshall Islands Government, 1996a: 46
11 ibid: 47
12 Census, 1988 in Marshall Islands Government, 1989
13 Keene, 1992: 13
14 ibid
15 UNDP, 1994: 75
16 Marshall Islands Government, 1989: 18
17 Hezel and Reafsnyder, 1988: 88
18 Trumbull,1977: 264
19 Marshall Islands Government, 1996: 40
20 Observed from the household listing for the 1992 Household Survey, OPS, cited in Marshall Islands Government, 1994
21 Marshall Islands Visitors Authority, 1997
22 UNICEF, 1996b: 6

CHAPTER 9

1   See examples in de Garine and Pollock, 1995
2   Defined as a body-mass index (BMI) of 20–25, see Bailey and Ferro-Luzzi, 1995
3   See examples in Mills (ed): 1988
4   Mull, 1991: 175–191
5   Simons, 1989: 132–146
6   For a summary of this debate see Caldwell, 1989: 101–111
7   This is a substantial overstatement (see Chapter 7) but a figure which was frequently mentioned by Marshallese not employed in the health sector
8   Maragos, 1994: 70
9   ibid: 55
10 UNDP, 1994: 46
11 Marshall Islands Government, MOHE, 1996: 58; Marshall Islands Government, MOHE, 1997: 25A
12 Rubenstein, 1992
13 Schoeffel, 1992: 241

14   ibid: 240
15   *Journal of Pacific Island Nutrition*, September 1997: 1
16   Simmons and Voyle, 1996: 103
17   S Bagnall, personal communication
18   Manning et al, 1991: 62, 86

References

Alfred, J (2000) 'Marshall Islands: It Isn't Getting Any Better', *Pacific Islands Nutrition*, Noumea: South Pacific Commission, June

Ambrose, S E (1993) *Rise to Globalism: American Foreign Policy Since 1938*, Harmondsworth: Penguin

Anderson, S and Staugard, F (1986) *Traditional Midwives*, Gaberone: Ipelegeng

Ashton, H and Stepney, R (1982) *Smoking*, London: Tavistock

Australian Institute of Health and Welfare (AIHW) (1996) *Australia's Health 1996*, Canberra: Australian Government Publishing Service

Bailey, K V and Ferro-Luzzi, A H (1995) 'Use of Body Mass Index of Adults in Assessing Individual and Community Nutritional Status', *Bulletin of the World Health Organization*, vol 73, no 5, pp 673–80

Bank of Hawaii (1992) 'Republic of the Marshall Islands', *Pacific Islands Economic Trends,* Report to the Business Opportunities Conference, Honolulu, January 16–17

Beck, U (1994) *Reflexive Modernisation: Politics, Tradition and Aesthetics in the Modern Social Order*, Cambridge: Polity

Becker, M H, Maiman, L A, Kirscht, J P, Haefner, D P and Drachman, R H (1977) 'The Health Belief Model and Prediction of Dietary Compliance: a Field Experiment', *Journal of Health and Social Behaviour*, vol 18, pp 348–66

Berg, J D (1988) *The Political Status of Palau and Nuclear Issues: Myth and Reality*, Washington DC, US State Department: Office of Freely Associated States

Black, D, Morris, D, Smith, C and Townshend, P (1982) *Inequalities in Health: the Black Report*, Middlesex: Penguin

Booth, H (1989) *Marshall Islands: A Statistical Profile on Men and Women*, Bangkok: UNDP/UNIFEM Pacific Mainstreaming Project

Brandt, W and The Independent Commission on International Development Issues (1980) *North–South: a Programme for Survival*, London: Pan

Bray, G A (ed) (1975) *Obesity in Perspective*, Washington DC: US Government Printing Office

Brewis, A, Schoeffel-Meleisea, P Mavoa, H and Maconaghie, K (1996) 'Gender and Non-communicable Diseases in the Pacific', *Pacific Health Dialog*, vol 3, no 1, pp 107–12

Briguglio, L (1995) 'Small Island Developing States and their Economic Vulnerabilities', *World Development*, vol 23, no 9, pp 1615–32

Brown, G W (1976) 'Social Causes of Disease', in Tuckett, D (ed) *An Introduction to Medical Sociology*, London: Tavistock, pp 291–333

Brown, G W and Harris, T (eds) (1989) *Life Events and Illness*, New York: Guilford Press

Brown, L (1974) *The Global Politics of Resource Scarcity*, Washington DC: Overseas Development Council

Buchanan, K (1985) 'Center and Periphery: Reflections on the Irrelevance of a Billion Human Beings', *Monthly Review*, New York, July/August, pp 86–97

Bushnell, O A (1993) *The Gifts of Civilization: Germs and Genocide in Hawaii*, Honolulu: University of Hawaii Press

Caldwell, J C (1989) 'Mass Education As a Determinant of Mortality Decline', Chapter 5 in J C Caldwell and G Santow (eds) *Selected Readings in the Cultural Social and Behavioural Determinants of Health*, Health Transition Series no 1, Canberra: Health Transition Centre, Australian National University, pp 101–11

Cameron, I (1987) *Lost Paradise*, London: Century Hutchinson

Cariceo, C (1994) 'Material Mortality in Mongolia: Cultural and Institutional Factors', Master of Social Work thesis, Graduate Programme in Social Work, York University, North York, Ontario, Canada

Carucci, L (1997) Nuclear Nativity: Rituals of Renewal and Empowerment in the Marshall Islands, Dekalb: Northern Illinois University Press

Centre for Co-operation with the Economies in Transition (1996) *Investment Guide for Uzbekistan*, Paris: OECD

Chapman, P L (ed) (1989) *Investor's Guide to The Republic of the Marshall Islands*, Washington DC: The Micronesia Institute

Chomsky, N (1993) *The Prosperous Few and the Restless Many: Noam Chomsky interviewed by D Barsamian*, Berkeley, California: Odonian Press

Chomsky, N and Herman, E S (1988) *Manufacturing Consent: The Political Economy of the Mass Media*, New York: Pantheon

Clark, R S and Sann, M (eds) (1996) *The Case Against the Bomb*, Camden, New Jersey: Rutgers University School of Law

Cohen, S, Evans, G W, Stokols, D and Krantz, D S (1986) *Behaviour, Health and Environmental Stress*, New York: Plenum

Collins, V R, Dowse, G and Zimmet, P (1996) 'Smoking Prevalence and Trends in the Pacific', *Pacific Health Dialog*, vol 3, no 1, pp 87–95

Collis, B (1997) 'Food Secrets For a Longer Life', *Focus*, pp 19–21

Connell, J (1991) 'The New Micronesia: Pitfalls and Problems of Dependent Development', *Pacific Studies*, vol 14, no 2, pp 87–120

Connell, J and Maata, M (1994) *Environmental Planning, Climate Change and Potential Sea Level Rise: Report on the Mission to the Republic of the Marshall Islands*, RMI National Archive

Corin, E (1994) 'The Social and Cultural Matrix of Health and Disease', Chapter 4 in R G Evans, M L Barer and T R Marmor (eds) *Why Are*

Some People Healthy and Others Are Not?: The Determinants of Health of Populations, New York: Alidine de Gruyter, pp 93–132

Cox, R W (1987) *Production, Power and World Order: Social Forces in the Making of History*, New York: Columbia University Press

Coyne, T with Badcock, J and Taylor, R (eds) (1984) *The Effect of Urbanisation and Western Diet on the Health of Pacific Island Populations*, Technical Paper no 186, Noumea: South Pacific Commission

Dahl, C (1996) 'Different Options, Different Paths: Economic Development in Two Atoll States', *ISLA: A Journal of Micronesian Studies*, vol 4, no 2, pp 289–316

Deloitte & Touche (1996a) *Independent Auditors' Report on the Independent Control Structure, Year ended September 30 1995*, Majuro: Deloitte & Touche

Deloitte & Touche (1996b) *Independent Auditors' Report on Compliance with Laws and Regulations, Year ended September 30 1995*, Majuro: Deloitte & Touche

Deloitte & Touche (1996c) *General Purpose Financial Statements and Independent Auditors' Report, Year ended September 30 1995*, Majuro: Deloitte & Touche

Demographic Health Surveys (DHS) (1996) *Uzbekistan Demographic and Health Survey 1996: Preliminary Report*, Maryland: Ministry of Health, Uzbekistan and Macro International

Denoon, D with Firth, S, Linnekin, J, Meleisa, M and Nero, K (eds) (1997) *The Cambridge History of the Pacific Islanders*, Cambridge: Cambridge University Press

Department of Environment, Sport and Territories (1995) *Active and Inactive Australians: Assessing and Understanding Levels of Physical Activity*, Canberra: Commonwealth of Australia

Diamond, I and McDonald, P (1994) 'Mortality', in D Lucas and P Meyer (eds) *Beginning Population Studies*, Canberra: The Australian National University, pp 29–43

Durkheim, E (ed) (1986) *Durkheim on Politics and the State*, with an introduction by A Giddens, Stanford, California: Stanford University Press

Ender, N S (1988) 'Hassles, Health and Happiness', in M P Janisse (ed) *Individual Differences, Stress, and Health Psychology*, New York: Springer-Verlag, pp 24–56

Evans, J (1992) *Transit of Venus*, New York: Pantheon Books

Evans, R G (1994) 'Introduction' in R G Evans, M L Barer, and T R Marmor (eds) (1994) *Why Are Some People Healthy and Others Are Not?: The Determinants of Health of Populations*, New York: Alidine de Gruyter, pp 3–26

Evans, R G and Stoddart, G L (1994) 'Producing Health, Consuming Health Care', Chapter 2 in R G Evans, M L Barer, and T R Marmor (eds) (1994) *Why Are Some People Healthy and Others Are Not?: The Determinants of Health of Populations*, New York: Alidine de Gruyter, pp 27–66

Falk, R, Kim, S and Mendlovitz, S (1982) *Toward a Just World Order*, Boulder: Westview

Fine, B (1998) *The Political Economy of Diet, Health and Food Policy*, London: Routledge

Finsch, O (1893) 'Ethnologische Erfahrungen und Belegstuche aus der Sudsee', Wein Yale University Translation, in L Mason (ed) *Selected Papers* (1947), Honolulu: University of Hawaii

Frank, A G (1978) *Dependent Accumulation and Underdevelopment*, London: Macmillan

Fukuyama, F (1992) *The End of History and the Last Man*, New York: Free Press

de Garine, I and Pollock, N (eds) (1995) *Social Aspects of Obesity*, South Australia: Gordon and Breach

George, S (1988) *A Fate Worse Than Debt*, Harmondsworth: Penguin

Goskomprognostat (Uzbekistan Government State Committee on Statistics and Forecasting) and Organisation for Economic Co-operation and Development (1995) *The Investment Guide for Uzbekistan*, OECD Working Paper, vol 3, no 39, Paris: OECD

Griffen, K (ed) (1995) *Social Policy and Economic Transformation in Uzbekistan*, Geneva: International Labour Organisation and United Nations Development Programme

Gunasekera, H M and Butuna, J B (1995) 'Population Growth and Economic Development Experience in the Republic of the Marshall Islands', Paper presented to the National Seminar on Population and Development in the Republic of the Marshall Islands', Majuro, 10–12 July

Hagen, E (1962) *On the Theory of Social Change: How Economic Growth Begins*, Homewood: Dorsey Press

Harpham, T (1994) 'Urbanisation and Mental Health in Developing Countries: A Research Role for Social Scientists, Public Health Professionals and Social Psychiatrists', *Social Science and Medicine*, vol 39, no 2, pp 233–45

Hart, R H, Besley, M A and Tarimo, E (1990) *Integrating Maternal and Child Health Services with Primary Health Care*, Geneva: World Health Organization

Heine, A (1984) 'Urbanization and Social Change in the Marshall Islands', *Ambio*, vol 13, no 5–6, pp 313–15

Heine, C (1974) *Micronesia at the Crossroads*, Honolulu: University of Hawaii Press

Hertzman, C, Frank, J and Evans, R G (1994) 'Heterogeneities in Health Status and the Determinants of Population Health', Chapter 3 in R G Evans, M L Barer and T R Marmor (eds) *Why Are Some People Healthy and Others Are Not?: The Determinants of Health of Populations*, New York: Alidine de Gruyter, pp 67–92

Hetland, H and Haycock, J (1995) 'Investment for Health', Chapter 6 in Griffen, K (ed) *Social Policy and Economic Transformation in*

Uzbekistan, Geneva: International Labour Organisation and United Nations Development Programme

Hetzel, B and McMichael, T (1987) *The LS Factor: Lifestyle and Health*, Ringwood, Australia: Penguin

Hezel, F X (1989) 'Suicide and the Micronesian Family', *The Contemporary Pacific*, vol 1, nos 1–2, pp 43–74

Hezel, F X and Reafsnyder, C B (1988 revised edition) *Micronesia: A Changing Society*, Truk: Micronesian Social Studies Program

Hobbes, T (1994) *Human Nature, or the Fundamental Elements of Policy*, with a new introduction by G A J Rogers, Bristol: Thoemmes

Hodge, A, Dowse, G and Zimmet, P (1996) 'Obesity in Pacific Populations', *Pacific Health Dialog* vol 3, no 1, pp 77–86

Humphrey, C and Sneath, D (eds) (1996) *Culture and Environment in Inner Asia*, vols 1 and 2, Cambridge: White Horse Press

Icke, D (1990) *It Doesn't Have to be This Way*, London, Green Print

Independent Commission on Population and Quality of Life (1996) *Caring for the Future: Making the Next Decades Provide a Life Worth Living*, Oxford: Oxford University Press

International Monetary Fund (1992) *Economic Review: Uzbekistan*, Washington DC: IMF

Jagchid, S and Hyer, P (1979) *Mongolia's Culture and Society*, Boulder: Westview Press

Johnson, G (1988) 'Marshall Islands: Politics in the Marshall Islands', in R Crocombe and L Mason (eds) *Micronesian Politics*, Suva: University of the South Pacific, pp 69–85

Journal of Pacific Island Nutrition (1997) Noumea: South Pacific Commission, September, p 1

Kabua, P and Pollock, N (1967) 'The ecological basis of political power in Laura Community', in *The Laura Report*, Hawaii: University of Hawaii Press, p 85

Kachondham, Y (1992) 'Report of a Consultancy on the Mongolian Child Nutrition Survey', unpublished report, UNICEF East Asia and Pacific Regional Office and UNICEF Ulaan Baatar

Kaser, M and Mehrotra, S (1992) *The Central Asian Economies After Independence*, London: Royal Institute of International Affairs

Keene, D (1992) 'Kokan: Youthful Female Runaways in the Marshall Islands', *Micronesia Counselor*, Occasional Papers, no 8, Chuuk: Federated States of Micronesia Mental Health Project

Kennedy, P (1989) *The Rise and Fall of the Great Powers: Economic Change and Military Conflict From 1500 to 2000*, London: Fontana

Keohane, R and Nye, J (1987) 'Power and Interdependence Revisited', *International Organisation*, vol 41, no 4, pp 725–53

Khan, M, Anker, R, Gosh Dastidar, S and Bairathi, S (1989) 'Inequalities Between Men and Women in Nutrition and Family Welfare Services: an In-depth Enquiry in an Indian Village', Chapter 10 in J Caldwell and G Santo (eds) *Selected Readings in the Cultural, Social and Behavioural*

Determinants of Health, Health Transition Series No 1, Canberra, Health Transition Centre, Australian National University, pp 175–99

King, J (1983) 'Attribution Theory and the Health Belief Model', in M Hewstone (ed) *Attribution Theory: Social and Functional Extensions*, Oxford: Blackwell

Kluge, P F (1991) *The Edge of Paradise: America in Micronesia*, New York: Random House

Kramer, A (1906) 'Hawaii Ostmikronesien und Samoa', Stuttgart, Yale University Translation, in L Mason (ed) *Selected Papers* (1947), Honolulu: University of Hawaii

Larkins, R G, Zimmet, P Z and Chisholm, D J (eds) (1989) *Diabetes 1988*, Amsterdam: Excerpta Medica

Lattimore, O (1955) *Nationalism and Revolution in Mongolia*, Leiden: E J Brill

Lutz, C A (1988) *Unnatural Emotions: Everyday Sentiments on a Micronesian Atoll and Their Challenge to Western Theory*, Chicago: University of Chicago Press

Machiavelli, N (1913) *The Prince*, 3rd edition, Oxford: Clarendon Press

Manning, W G, Keeler, E B, Newhouse, J P, Sloss, E M and Wasserman, J (1991) *The Costs of Poor Health Habits*, Massachusetts: Harvard University Press

Maragos, J E (1994) 'Description of Reefs and Corals for the 1988 Protected Area Survey of the Northern Marshall Islands', *Atoll Research Bulletin*, no 419, pp 1–84

Marmot, M and Wadsworth, M E J (eds) (1997) 'Fetal and Early Childhood Environment: Long-Term Health Implications', *British Medical Bulletin*, Special issue, vol 53, no 1

Marmot, M and Wilkinson, R G (1999) *Social Determinants of Health*, Oxford: Oxford University Press

Marshall Islands Government (1988) *Statistical Abstract of the Marshall Islands 1987*, Majuro: Office of Planning and Statistics

Marshall Islands Government (1989) *Census of Population and Housing 1988: Final Report*, Majuro: Office of Planning and Statistics, Republic of the Marshall Islands

Marshall Islands Government (1990) *National Population Policy*, Majuro: Office of Planning and Statistics, Republic of the Marshall Islands

Marshall Islands Government (1991) *The Republic of The Marshall Islands National Nutrition Survey*, Majuro: Ministry of Health Services, Republic of the Marshall Islands

Marshall Islands Government (1994) *Republic of the Marshall Islands Statistical Abstract 1992*, Majuro: Office of Planning and Statistics, Republic of the Marshall Islands

Marshall Islands Government (1995) *National Women's Policy, Republic of the Marshall Islands 1966–2001*, Majuro: Ministry of Social Services, Republic of the Marshall Islands

Marshall Islands Government (1996a) *1995 Annual Report; Implementation of the Compact of Free Association for Fiscal Year*

1995, Majuro: Presented to the President of the United States and Congress of the United States of America by the Nitijela

Marshall Islands Government (1996b) *Annual Report to the Nitijela for the Calendar Year 1996*, Majuro: Nuclear Claims Tribunal, Republic of the Marshall Islands

Marshall Islands Government (1996c) *Marshall Islands Vital and Health Statistics Abstract*, Majuro: Bureau of Health Planning and Statistics, Republic of the Marshall Islands

Marshall Islands Government (1997) *Twenty-sixth Semi Annual Report of the Functions and Activities of the Office of the Auditor General, August 1st to December 31st, 1996 (2 Volumes)*, Majuro: Submitted to the Nitijela 18th Constitutional Regular Session, 1997

Marshall Islands Government (1997 Draft) *Reporting Status or Progress: Ministry of Health and Environment Annual Report FY96*, Majuro: Bureau of Health Planning and Statistics, Republic of the Marshall Islands

Marshall Islands Government (2000) *1999 Census of Population and Housing: Final Report*, Majuro: Office of Planning and Statistics

Marshall Islands Visitors Authority (1997) *RMI Country Profile and Visitors Guide*, Majuro: Marshall Islands Visitors Authority

Mason, L (1989) 'A Marshallese nation emerges from the political fragmentation of American Micronesia', *Pacific Studies*, vol 13, no 1, pp1–46

McArthur, N (1967) *Island Populations of the Pacific*, London: Hurst

McHenry, D F (1975) *Micronesia: Trust Betrayed, Altruism vs Self Interest in American Foreign Policy*, New York: Carnegie Endowment for International Peace

McMurray, C (1995) 'Report on the Republic of the Marshall Islands Fertility and Family Planning Survey, November–December', unpublished report, Majuro: Office of Planning and Statistics, Republic of the Marshall Islands

Medvedeva, T (1996) 'Medical Services and Health Issues in Rural Areas of Inner Asia', in C Humphrey and D Sneath (eds) *Culture and Environment in Inner Asia*, vols 1 and 2, Cambridge: White Horse Press, pp 176–204

Mellor, N (1985) *Constitutionalism in Micronesia*, Honolulu: University of Hawaii Press

Merlin, M, Capelle, A, Keene, T, Juvik, J and Maragos, J (1994) *Plants and Environments of the Marshall Islands*, Hawaii: East West Center

Merton, R K (1957) *Social Theory and Social Structure*, revised edition, Glencoe, Illinois: Free Press of Glencoe

Merton, R K and Chirot, D (1986) *Social Change in the Modern Era*, San Diego: Harcourt Brace Jovanovich

Micronesia Support Committee (1983) *Marshall Islands A Chronology: 1944–1983*, Honolulu, Hawaii: Micronesia Support Committee

Micronitor News and Printing Company (1996) *Nuclear Testing in the Marshall Islands: A Brief History*, Majuro: Micronitor News and Printing Company

Millard, A V, Ferguson, A E and Khaila, S W (1990) 'Agricultural Development and Malnutrition: a Causal Model of Child Mortality', in J C Caldwell, S Findley, P Caldwell, G Santow, W Cosford, J Braid and D Broers-Fraeman (eds) *What We Know About Health Transition*, Proceedings of an International Workshop, Canberra, May, 1989, Health Transition Series no 2, Canberra: Health Transition Centre, Australian National University, pp 285–310

Mills, S (ed) (1988) *Alternatives in Healing: an Open-minded Approach to Finding the Best Treatment for Your Health Problems*, London: Macmillan

Mogensen, C E and Standl, E (eds) (1991) *Pharmacology of Diabetes: Present Practice and Future Perspectives*, Berlin: Walter de Gruyter

Mongolian Government (1993) *Health Statistics of Mongolia, 1960–1992*, Ulaanbaatar: Ministry of Health

Mongolian Government (1994) *Population of Mongolia*, Ulaanbaatar: State Statistical Office of Mongolia

Morgenthau, H J (1978) *Politics Among Nations: the Struggle for Power and Peace*, New York: Alfred A Knopf

Mull, D S (1991) 'Traditional Perceptions of Marasmus in Pakistan', *Social Science and Medicine*, vol 32, no 2, pp 175–91

Murai, M (1954) 'Nutrition Study of Micronesia', *Atoll Research Bulletin*, Washington: The Pacific Science Board

Myrdal, G (1953) *The Political Element in the Development of Economic Theory*, London: Routledge and Kegan Paul

National Marine Fisheries Service (1985) *Potential for Fisheries Development in the Marshall Islands*, US Department of Commerce, Washington: International Development Cooperation Agency

Neupert, R (1995) 'Early-age Mortality, Socio-economic Development and the Health System in Mongolia', *Health Transition Review*, vol 5, no 1, April, pp 44–8

Neupert, R (1996) *Population Policies, Socioeconomic Development and Population Dynamics in Mongolia*, Canberra: Research School of Social Sciences, Australian National University

Nufer, H (1978) *Micronesia Under American Rule*, Hicksville: Exposition

Ogden, M R (1994) 'MIRAB and The Marshall Islands', *ISLA: A Journal of Micronesian Studies*, vol 2, no 2, pp 237–72

Omran, A R and Strandley, C (eds) (1976) *Family Formation Patterns and Health: An International Collaborative Study in India, Iran, Lebanon, Philippines and Turkey*, Geneve: WHO

Onon, U and Pritchatt, D (1989) *Asia's First Modern Revolution: Mongolia Proclaims its Independence in 1911*, Leiden: E J Brill

Ordung, N (1996) 'Enhancement of Social Security for the Poor: the Case Study of Uzbekistan', unpublished consultant's report, Tashkent, Uzbekistan: Economic Institute

Organisation for Economic Co-operation and Development (1996) *Investment Guide for Uzbekistan*, Paris: OECD

Osmani, S R (1992) 'On Some Controversies in the Measurement of Undernutrition', in S R Osmani (ed) *Nutrition and Poverty*, Oxford: Clarendon Press, pp 121–64

Pacific News Bulletin (1988) February–March, p 5, Pacific Concerns Resource Centre, Suva, Fiji

Parsons, C (1985) *Healing Practices in the South Pacific*, Hawaii: Institute for Polynesian Studies

Peattie, M (1992) *Nanjo: The Rise and Fall of the Japanese in Micronesia, 1885–1945*, Honolulu: University of Hawaii Press

Pietrzik, K (1991) *Modern Lifestyles, Lower Energy Intake and Micronutrient Status*, London: Springer-Verlag

Pollock, N J (1974) 'Breadfruit or Rice: Dietary Choice on a Micronesian Atoll', *Ecology of Food and Nutrition*, vol 3, pp 107–15

Preston, S H (1989) 'Resources, Knowledge and Child Mortality: A Comparison of the US in the Late Nineteenth Century and Developing Countries Today', in J C Caldwell and M G Santow (eds) *Selected Readings in the Cultural, Social and Behavioural Determinants of Health* Health Transition Series no 1, Canberra: Health Transition Centre, Australian National University, pp 66–78

Purcell, D (1976) 'The Economics of Exploitation: the Japanese in Mariana, Caroline and Marshall Islands, 1915–1940', *Journal of Pacific History*, vol 11, no 3, pp 189–211

Raharjo, Y and Corner, L (1990) 'Cultural Attitudes to Health and Sickness in Public Health Programs: a Demand-creation Approach Using Data from West Aceh, Indonesia', in Caldwell et al (eds) *What We Know About Health Transition*, proceedings of an international workshop, Canberra, May 1989, Health Transition Series No 2, Canberra: Health Transition Centre, Australian National University

Richard, D E (1957) *United States Naval Administration of the Trust Territories of the Pacific Islands*, Washington DC: Office of the Chief of Naval Operations

Roberts, K J (1995) 'Ethnicity and Social Distance in the Marshall Islands', paper presented at the Ethnicity and Multi-ethnicity Conference, Hawaii: Brigham Young University

Robertson, R (1992) *Globalisation, Social Theory and Global Culture*, London: Sage

Rosenstrater, L (1996) *Aquaculture Feasibility Study: Environmental Resources on Two Outer Islands*, University of Oregon, Micronesian and South Pacific Program

Royston, E and Anderson, S (1989) *Preventing Maternal Deaths*, Geneva: World Health Organization

Rubenstein, D (ed) (1992) *Pacific History: Papers from the 8th Pacific History Association Conference*, Mangilao, Guam: University of Guam and the Micronesian Area Research Center

Runeborg, R (1980) *The Marshall Islands: History, Culture and Communication*, Honolulu: East-West Communications Institute

Rupen, R (1979) *How Mongolia is Really Ruled: A Political History of the Mongolian People's Republic, 1900–1978*, Stanford, California: Hoover Institution Press

Rusman, R (1999) *They Simply Die: Searching for the Causes of High Infant Mortality in Lombok*, Jakarta: PPT-LIPI

Ruvussin, E, Valencia, M E and Schultz, L O (1994) 'Effects of Traditional Lifestyle on Obesity in Pima Indians', *Diabetes Care*, vol 17, no 9

Schoeffel, P (1992) 'Food Health and Development in the Pacific Islands: Policy Implications for Micronesia', *ISLA: A Journal of Micronesian Studies*, vol 1, no 2, Dry Season, pp 223–50

Simmons, D and Voyle, J A (1996) 'Psychosocial and Behavioural Aspects of NIDDM Among Pacific Islanders in South Auckland', *Pacific Health Dialog*, vol 3, no 1, pp 100–6

Simons, J (1989) 'Cultural Dimensions of the Mother's Contribution to Child Survival', Chapter 7 in J C Caldwell and G Santow (eds) *Selected Readings in the Cultural Social and Behavioural Determinants of Health*, Health Transition Series no 1, Canberra: Health Transition Centre, Australian National University, pp 132–46

Smith, R (1997) *The Nuclear Free and Independent Pacific Movement: After Moruroa*, London: Tauris Academic Studies

Soucie, E A (1983) *Atoll Agriculture for Secondary Schools: Soils and Major Agricultural Crops of Micronesia*, Ponape: Ponape Agricultura and Trade School

Spennemann, D H R (1992) 'Makmok: Polynesian Arrowroot in the Marshall Islands', Occasional Papers in Traditional Food Crops, Majuro: RMI Ministry of Internal Affairs

Spennemann, D H R (1996) 'Nontraditional Settlement Patterns and Typhoon Hazard on Contemporary Majuro Atoll, Republic of the Marshall Islands', *Environmental Management*, vol 20, no 3, pp 337–48

Spielberger, C D, Krasner, S S and Solomon, E P (1988) 'The Experience, Expression and Control of Anger', in M P Janisse (ed) *Individual Differences, Stress, and Health Psychology*, New York: Springer-Verlag, pp 89–108

Sprout, M (1985) *Review of Agricultural Program Procedures and Methods: Survey of Agricultural Islands, Enewatek Atoll, Marshall Islands*, RMI National Archive

Sterling, T D, Rosenbaum, W L and Weinkam, J J (1993) 'Risk Attribution and Tobacco-related Deaths', *American Journal of Epidemiology*, vol 138, no 2, pp 128–39

Strange, S (1996) *The Retreat of the State: the Diffusion of Power in the World Economy*, New York: Cambridge University Press

Timberlake, L (1985) *Africa in Crisis: the Causes, the Cures of Environmental Bankruptcy*, edited by Jon Tinker, London: Earthscan/International Institute for Environment and Development

Tomlinson, J (1991) *Cultural Imperialism: a Critical Introduction*, London: Pinter

Trumbull, R (1977) *Tin Roofs and Palm Trees: a Report on the New South Seas*, Canberra: ANU Press

UNDP (1991) *Towards Sustainable Development for Atolls and Other Small Islands: IADP's Institution Building and Replication Phase*, Suva: UNDP

UNDP (1994) *Pacific Human Development Report*, Suva: UNDP

UNDP (1995) *Uzbekistan Human Development Report 1995*, Tashkent: UNDP

UNDP (1997a) *Pelaak*, vol 1, issue 1, UNDP RMI Coastal Management Program for Majuro Atoll

UNDP (1997b) *Human Development Report 1997*, Oxford: Oxford University Press

UNDP (1997c) *Human Development Report Mongolia 1997*, Ulaanbaatar: UNDP

UNDP/ILO (1995) *Social Policy and Economic Transformation in Uzbekistan*, Geneva: International Labour Organisation

UNDP (1996a) *Uzbekistan Human Development Report*, Tashkent: UNDP

UNDP (1996b) *Human Development Report 1996*, Oxford: Oxford University Press

UNFPA (1997) *The State of World Population*, New York: UNFPA

UNICEF (1990) *An Analysis of the Situation of Children and Women in Mongolia*, New Delhi: UNICEF

UNICEF (1994) *The State of the World's Children 1994*, Oxford: Oxford University Press

UNICEF (1996a) *The State of the World's Children 1996*, Oxford: Oxford University Press

UNICEF (1996b) *A Situation Analysis of Children and Women in the Marshall Islands 1996*, Suva: UNICEF

United Nations (1982) *Levels and Trends of Mortality since 1950*, New York: Department of International Economic and Social Affairs

United Nations (1996) *Levels and Trends of Contraceptive Use as Assessed in 1994*, New York: Population Division

US Peace Corps Volunteers (1986) *The Republic of the Marshall Islands: An Emerging Nation*, Columbia, Maryland: Development Through Self-Reliance

Wallerstein, I and Hopkins, T (1996) *The Age of Transition: Trajectory of the World System, 1945–2025*, London: Zed Books

Weisgall, J (1994) *Operation Crossroads: The Atomic Tests at Bikini Atoll*, Annapolis, Maryland: Naval Institute Press

Wiseman, J (ed) (1997) *Alternatives to Globalisation: An Asia-Pacific Perspective*, Fitzroy: Community Aid Abroad

World Bank (1993) 'Marshall Islands' Volume 4 of *Pacific Island Economies: Towards Efficient Sustainable Growth*, Country Economic Memorandum, Washington: The World Bank

World Health Organization (1946) Constitution of the WHO, reprinted in *Basic Documents*, 37th edn, Geneva: WHO

World Health Organization (1990) *Diet, Nutrition and the Prevention of Chronic Diseases*, WHO Technical Report Series no 797, Geneva: WHO
Youth to Youth in Health (1997) *Program Report 1995–96*, Majuro: Youth to Youth in Health
Zuckerman, M (1988) 'Sensation Seeking, Risk Taking, and Health', in M P Janisse (ed) *Individual Differences, Stress, and Health Psychology*, New York: Springer-Verlag, pp 72–88

Index